"This book, grounded in more than a decade of partnership work, offers compelling ethical and practical guidance to scholars seeking to learn how to engage in community-based participatory research that embodies a pluralistic stance toward knowledge-building and that works toward educational justice. Its detailed portraits of meeting agendas, dilemmas and ideological tensions of research practice, and jointly constructed artifacts of inquiry provide exemplary models for how to center care, relationship, and justice in research."

—William Penuel, Distinguished Professor, Learning Sciences and
Human Development, University of Colorado Boulder, USA

"I cannot imagine a more indispensable resource for community-based scholarship! Drawing on rich theory and community knowledges, engrossing narratives, and detailed examples and photos, the authors elaborate the complexities, relationalities, and profound ontologies of collaborative inquiry between university-based researchers, youth, families, communities, and educators. They bring the often-abstract dimensions of partnering with communities to life with piercing, vulnerable insights from their longstanding efforts to realize research methodologies of love in pursuit of pluralistic knowledge and tangible change with and in communities. If you have ever wondered how research might transform its extractive, colonizing legacy to reckon with power, live radical solidarity, and imagine different worlds in the making, look no further than this book to light our way forward!"

—Ann Ishimaru, Killinger Endowed Chair & Professor, Educational
Foundations, Leadership & Policy, College of Education at the
University of Washington, USA

"Methods for Community-Based Research: Advancing Educational Justice and Epistemic Rights is a book for our times. As more communities demand research be conducted "with" rather than "on" them, Ghiso and Campano illuminate the way forward. This book is a compass for fostering collaboration between researchers and communities, paving the way to a more just education system. Through compelling research, this text showcases the transformative power of Community-Based Research, emphasizing community involvement, cultural sensitivity, and empowerment as the cornerstones of change. Ghiso and Campano show that CBRE is more than a methodology; it's a philosophy that respects the wisdom and agency of those most impacted by educational inequities. This book is a guide to conducting research that is not only respectful and inclusive but also effective."

—Yolanda Sealey-Ruiz, Professor of English Education, Teachers College,
Columbia University, USA

D1559476

Methods for Community-Based Research

Methods for Community-Based Research describes how Community-Based Research (CBR) is particularly suited to understand and take action on issues of educational justice.

The book shifts assumptions about who is considered a researcher, drawing attention to issues of power and the ethics of collaborations, and foregrounding how those who have often been positioned as the objects of educational interventions can—and have the rights to—play an active role in creating educational arrangements more conducive to their own flourishing. The authors draw on a decade-long partnership across the boundaries of race, language, immigration status, and institutional affiliation to provide examples that illustrate the complexities and possibilities of this work. They distill principles, practices, and ongoing inquiries for researchers to consider across all aspects of the research process.

The book supports researchers in creating the conditions for collaborative inquiry into issues of educational (in)justice that are salient to community partners. It will be of interest to advanced undergraduate, graduate students and scholars in education, and other disciplines that utilize a CBR method such as healthcare research and anthropology, as well as scholars interested in qualitative methods and issues of social justice in research.

María Paula Ghiso is Professor of Literacy Education in the Department of Curriculum and Teaching at Teachers College, Columbia University in New York City, USA.

Gerald Campano is Professor of Literacy Studies at the University of Pennsylvania Graduate School of Education in Philadelphia, PA, USA.

Methods for Community-Based Research

Advancing Educational Justice and Epistemic Rights

María Paula Ghiso and Gerald Campano

Routledge
Taylor & Francis Group

LONDON AND NEW YORK

Designed cover image: Malia Kealaluhi

First published 2024
by Routledge
4 Park Square, Milton Park, Abingdon, Oxon OX14 4RN

and by Routledge
605 Third Avenue, New York, NY 10158

Routledge is an imprint of the Taylor & Francis Group, an informa business

British Library Cataloguing-in-Publication Data
A catalogue record for this book is available from the British Library

ISBN: 978-1-032-24665-9 (hbk)
ISBN: 978-1-032-24667-3 (pbk)
ISBN: 978-1-003-27968-6 (ebk)

DOI: 10.4324/9781003279686

Typeset in Optima
by Newgen Publishing UK

Contents

Foreword

The intersecting crises of our time – including rising white nationalism, exclusionary borders, globalized racial capitalism, pervasive anti-blackness, environmental devastation – continue to generate cycles of dehumanization, labor exploitation, displacement, detention, and deportation. The world is in dire need of listeners, artists, filmmakers, writers, litigators, healers, organizers, and educators who can practice situated solidarities and leverage their gifts for the co-creation of more just and precious worlds. Through testimonies of prolonged relationality, *Methods for Community-Based Research: Advancing Educational Justice and Epistemic Rights* reminds us that the stewarding of knowledge is always ubiquitous and abundant beyond the narrow walls of academia.

The CARE Partnership featured in this book is an example of how community-based research in education (CBRE) can foster "un mundo donde quepan muchos mundos" (a world where many worlds can co-exist), which, borrowing from the Ejercito Zapatista de Liberación Nacional (EZLN; National Zapatista Liberation Army), signals a "pluri-versal world" or a "pluri-versality as a universal project" (Mignolo, 2007, p. 452). The authors argue that relationships are not defined by a short-term grant or extractive knowledge-mining from university researchers and instead highlight what can happen when community members – elders and young people alike – are (re)positioned as co-theorizers that steward knowledge collectively over long periods of time. Latina feminist scholar Gilda Ochoa (2022) has noted the danger of researchers "parachut[ing] from one community and topic to another" where "ties are construed as temporary and utilitarian until researchers advance to the next project" (Ochoa, 2022, p. 253). In contrast to extractive approaches, the book's advancement of CBRE prioritizes experiential knowledge for tackling problems caused by unequal and harmful social and political systems, and for envisioning and implementing alternatives that are longstanding. Across the chapters, the authors detail how they have carefully and thoughtfully incorporated the participation and leadership of marginalized community members, how said partners have taken action to produce emancipatory social change, and how they have conducted systematic research together that has generated socially transformative new knowledge.

Approaching the thirtieth anniversary of the Zapatista uprising from the Chiapas Lacandon jungle of México, the primarily Indigenous Maya women leaders of the EZLN have been influential globally in their organizing and resistance through autonomy as a response to injustices generated by neo-liberalism in the twentieth century. As a social movement, the EZLN prioritizes the dignity of Indigenous racialized "others," belonging, and common struggle, as well as the importance of laughter, joy, and the emotional and educa-tional wellbeing of their entire communities. Some of the key features of the CARE Partnership are reminiscent of what Holloway (2005) has called "urban Zapatismo," or the ways that metropolitan city organizers and educators are "caminando preguntando," bringing notions of self-determination, praxis, and autonomy to their creating of other possible worlds. The classic Zapatista teaching, "la dignidad no se estudia, se vive o se muere, se duele en el pecho y enseña a caminar" (EZLN Communiqué, 1995) is also of great relevance to CBRE. Relational research is the embodiment of everyday practices of *lived dignity*, anchored in humanity, and is something that guides one's walking alongside others in the world. Through this book's attention to the dignity of all those involved, including the migrant and "other" in society, it reminds educators of the here-and-now sensibilities of ethical partnered research and racialized communities' engagements with social change from below (de los Ríos & Molina, 2020).

Rather than a blueprint for CBRE, the authors lead with cultural humility to advance a set of questions and principles that are critical for the inquiring of both self and other as racialized subjects, larger sociopolitical ecosystems, and the complexities entangled in the research process. Moreover, at a time when scholars are pressed to read the sheer *absences* of positionality and relationality across educational research (de los Ríos & Patel, 2023), even in studies marked as "critical research," this book is a rich and compelling example of the contrary.

Cati V. de los Ríos
Associate Professor of Literacy and Bi/Multilingual Education
School of Education, University of California, Berkeley

References

EZLN Communiqué (1995). Retrieved from http://palabra.ezln.org.mx/comunicados/1995/1995_06_20_b.htm

de los Ríos, C.V., & Molina, A. (2020). Literacies of refuge: "Pidiendo posada" as ritual of justice. *Journal of Literacy Research*, *51*(1), 32–54.

de los Ríos, C.V., & Patel, L. (2023). Positions, positionality, and relationality in educa-tional research. *International Journal of Qualitative Studies in Education*. https://doi.org/10.1080/09518398.2023.2268036

Holloway, J. (2005). Zapatista urbano. *Humboldt Journal of Social Relations, 29*(1), 168–178.

Mignolo, W. (2007). Delinking. *Cultural Studies, 21*(2), 449–514. http://dx.doi.org/10.1080/09502380601162647

Ochoa, G. (2022). Learning and being in community: A Latina feminist holistic approach to researching where we live. *International Journal of Research & Method in Education, 45*(3), 246–258.

Acknowledgments

In a discussion of how readers might encounter art, and how they might civically engage the world, the novelist and cultural critic Elaine Castillo demystifies the imperial impulse to understand ourselves as "sole, free actors in the world" and suggests, instead, that we know our individual selves "as one small flawed part of a whole" (Castillo, p. 73). As scholars we find this insight liberating, despite professional pressures to be authoritative. It is an acknowledgment simply of our humanity and a reminder that we are not alone in our respective imperfections. We are in this world together, implicated in one another's lives and part of a shared inheritance. The presumption of imperfection nurtures our faith in the collective brilliance of the community, where we learn, grow, and find hope.

The "whole" in the Communities Advancing Research in Education (CARE) Initiative, the inspiration for this book, is not an abstraction. It is composed of all the individuals who have given precious time out of their lives to show up for one another. Many have been central to the work throughout its over decade-long duration. Some have been involved on a more limited basis. Everyone's contributions have been a gift and singularly invaluable.

We are indebted to the following people who have helped the CARE Initiative come into fruition and continue to blossom: Danielle Ashley, Stefanie A., Dee Asaah, Ore Badaki, Katrina Bartow Jacobs, Alejanda Cabrales, Angela Chan, Wei Chen, Kenny Chiu, Yvonne Colson, Laura Colville, America Delcruz, Chinh Dinh, Jonathan Djoenadi, Esmeralda Fávila, Victoria Gill, Maria Goretti, Marco Kosasih, Rita Gracián, Frianna Gultom, Faustine Gultom, Jason Harianto, Taylor Hauburg, Sara Herlands, María Hernández, Alexa Hernandez Diaz, Frederick Hidayat, Chloe Kannan, Krithi Kannan, Paige Kaszuba, Sandra Kawulsan, Brenda Krishanwongso, Joseph Kwee, Vincenzio Kwee, Sophia Lauwidjaja, Robert LeBlanc, Minghui Li, Daby Lie, Putraka Lie, Jenny Lie, Jasmine Lie, Mengran Liu, Claudio Lorenzo, Chris Lorenzo, David Low, Quinn Luong, Jeannette Moon, Karim Mostafa, Larry Narron, Lan Ngo, Phil Nichols, Roch Parayre, Odalys Peralta, Erick Pérez, Itzel Pérez, Liz Pérez, Laura Peynado Castro, Fernanda Pilar, Lluli Pilar, Grace Player, Olivia Ponce, Emiliano Ponce Fávila, Martin Ponce Fávila, Martin Ponce Sr, Yared Portillo,

Alicia Rusoja, Alan S., Astrid Sambolín Morales, Yolanda Sanchez, Wendy Sanchez, Endang Santoso, Emily Rose Schwab, Christopher Schwarting, Yolanda Sealy-Ruiz, Patricia Sengbounpheng, Owen Setiawan, David Setiawan, Rob Simon, Claire So, Ericka Staufert-Reyes, Gwyneth Stevanus, Cherlyn Sukwanputra, Ellyana Sukwanputra, Jaqueline Sulwanputra, Timothy Sunton, Zion Sykes, Summer Sykes, Michelle Tan, Agus Tan, Alvert Tanjaya, Ankhi Thakurta, Raul Torres, Olivia Vazquez Ponce, Sina Ward, Michael Ward, Daria Ward, Bethany Welch, Andre Wijaya, Jackie Winsch, Gregory Wolmart, Tarajean Yazzie-Mintz, Mary Yee, and Boris Zhinin. We would also like to thank the editorial team from Routledge, including Eleanor Taylor, Matt Bickerton, and Hannah Shakespeare.

The research for this book has been supported by funding from a Spencer Foundation Research-Practice Partnership Grant, an American Educational Research Association's Educational Research Service Projects Grant, and an Equity in Research-Practice Partnerships Grant from the Spencer and William T. Grant Foundations. We are grateful that these organizations have recognized and given legitimacy to partnership research, which, for so much of our academic careers, has been an uphill journey driven primarily by passion and conviction. They have also provided a restorative space for kindred intellectual spirits to convene and learn from one another.

Reference

Castillo, E. (2022). *How to read now: Essays*. Viking Press.

1 Community-Based Research in the Service of Educational Transformation

What role can the educational research process itself play in addressing educational inequities? And who has a say in determining the focus of educational research, how it is carried out, and what impacts it engenders? Too often, examinations of educational challenges and proposed solutions are removed from the on-the-ground experiences of students, families, classroom teachers, and neighborhood leaders, who are seen as targets of educational interventions. A Community-Based Research in Education (CBRE) paradigm disrupts top-down transmission models of knowledge and positions communities as partners in research directed toward educational transformation. This book explores what happens when families and university-based researchers partner to investigate and take action on issues of educational justice. In doing so, we discuss salient methodological questions and topics related CBRE and educational research more broadly.

CBRE is a methodology which is driven by the questions and aspirations of those most impacted by educational inequities and those who work in solidarity with them. This approach is premised on the idea that some of the most important advances in education are the result of collective work as people come together across social and institutional boundaries in a spirit of epistemic cooperation. Our understanding of CBRE draws inspiration from the civic engagement and agency of Black, Brown, and immigrant communities who advocate for better lives and educational opportunities for future generations. Learning from the knowledge of local groups is paramount to developing more just learning spaces. CBRE has diverse scholarly roots and precedents, but its potentials will be realized in the creative collective alchemy occurring in singular contexts of intellectual inquiry and activism. As such, who the people engaging in inquiry are and what place they are doing it from matter to the direction and form of the research.

This is therefore not a "how to" book on research methodology advocating for an approach that can be standardized across contexts. It is structured as a series of inquiries meant to raise questions for your own sites of research and practice, where the nuances of context and relations are vital to the work. Every step of the research process requires attention to issues of ethics and power

DOI: 10.4324/9781003279686-1

to ensure community members are genuine co-designers and co-producers of research (Bang et al., 2015; Ishimaru & Bang, 2022). Throughout our book we draw on examples from our own 12-year partnership between ourselves (university faculty), university students, and Philadelphia families, many of whom are affiliated with a Catholic parish, school, and community center in South Philadelphia and self-identify as Black, Indonesian, Latine,[1] Irish, and Indigenous. We have come to call this work the Communities Advancing Research in Education (CARE) Initiative, an interracial and intergenerational community think tank investigating issues of educational access and justice. From the very beginning, the project has been intentional about including parents, caretakers, and community elders in participatory research—not just youth—because there are longstanding colonial histories in education of separating and alienating students from their families. This has had more obvious manifestations, such as in the genocidal abduction and forced assimilation of Native children to Indian Boarding Schools, but can also be perpetuated in more subtle ways, such as when schools reinforce border surveillance ideologies (Nuñez, 2021). The primary allegiance in CBRE is, by definition, to families and communities. It strives to honor the agency of families as they advocate for their children across social boundaries and political borders (Oliveira, 2018).

CBRE is profoundly (trans)local work. This is not to suggest that the research is somehow smaller or only has immediate impact. Rather, it involves a recognition that there is no Archimedean point from which to analyze that world, and it embraces that research is a process of inquiry situated in a specific set of relations: relations to others, to a place, to institutions, and to the environment. For example, in the CARE Initiative, each respective cultural, racialized, and linguistic group's rich historical legacies of resistance, survival, and thriving inform the nature of the research. It has mattered that this work began in a faith-based organization but has also grown beyond. It matters that the research involves families from Philadelphia, who encounter one of the most under-resourced school districts in the country but are also heirs to the city's ongoing history of organizing and rebellion. And, importantly, everyone who has been involved in the CARE Initiative is invaluable, with their own unique constellation of talents, perspectives, forms of affective involvement, and knowledge they have contributed to the partnership.

Each CBRE project is thus different and not replicable. Part of the challenge and reward of CBRE involves cultivating an appreciation for and mobilizing the collective genius of local relations. While we do not claim exhaustive knowledge or any kind of final word on CBRE, we do believe it is a form of critical and culturally relevant inquiry that is never "mastered." Nevertheless, this book could not have been written earlier in our careers. It is the result of our own ongoing inquiry stance (Cochran-Smith & Lytle, 2009), often in the face of dominant institutional research paradigms that devalue the work as merely "service" or "applied research." In the process of having to argue for and make space for CBRE, we have had to engage in a form of resistant theorizing, making the road by walking it, while learning from and being inspired by participatory intellectual traditions.

Yet a confluence of social and institutional currents suggest that the time is ripe for CBRE to gain a more prominent place in academia. Over the past decade, with the emergence of critical university studies, institutions of higher education are reflecting on their complicity in histories of oppression, which include exploitive research agendas and relations with their surrounding communities. This reflection is the result of pressure by community organizers and activists who—to invoke the disability rights movement—demand "nothing about us without us" and "we are our own best advocates" (e.g., Rusoja, 2022). Driven by these efforts, individualist and top-down approaches to educational research may be beginning to change. There have been increasing calls to bridge the gap between university research and the pressing educational problems impacting schools and communities through research-practice partnerships (RPPs). We consider CBRE to be one variety of research-practice partnerships, and we have been fortunate to be in conversation with colleagues in the field who have been at the forefront of this paradigmatic shift in education to democratize knowledge production (Coburn & Penuel, 2016), which has received support from major foundations and has most recently culminated in the inaugural *Handbook on Improvement-Focused Educational Research* (Peurach et al., 2022).

At the same time, a grounding in critical university studies reminds us to view the idea of "university-community partnerships" cautiously. Partnerships can reproduce existing hierarchies between universities and their surrounding neighborhoods. CBRE can play an important role in helping to shift assumptions about who is thought of as a researcher, drawing attention to issues of power and the ethics of collaboration, and foregrounding how those who have often been positioned as the objects of educational interventions can—and have the right to—play an active role in creating educational arrangements more conducive to their own flourishing. We thus believe that this book might offer insights to any researchers interested in educational equity and more just methods.

How We Became Involved in CBRE

Many of the topics we discuss in this book grew out of our early professional experiences as educators and literacy researchers interested in classroom practice. We entered graduate school as former full-time teachers who had developed a skepticism of standardized mandates, often espoused by policy makers or academics who themselves had never taught. We were fortunate to find a doctoral program that did not ask us to shed our identities as teachers, or cultural beings for that matter, to become researchers. In fact, we were encouraged by our graduate school mentors, including Susan L. Lytle, Vivian L. Gadsden, and Brian Street, to bring the insights derived from our teaching experiences and lives into our studies and how we envisioned our scholarship. Inspired by the teacher research movement, we returned to the classroom for our respective dissertation studies. María Paula investigated early-childhood writing and Gerald researched his own practice as a 5th-grade teacher. We viewed the students as members of our communities of inquiry, genuine intellectual interlocutors who had important knowledge to contribute. We strove to create a greater flow of dialogue between our respective schools and the surrounding communities. We were committed to critical, culturally relevant, and anti-oppressive approaches to teaching and learning. And, with the support of our mentors, we interrogated the relationship between theory and practice, with the idea that a more intimate dynamic between the two might help us reimagine educational research.

When we moved back to Philadelphia to accept academic positions on the East Coast, we had initially intended to work alongside city public school teachers but encountered a moratorium in the district on university-based research. We thus decided to take time to learn about the activist landscape of the city, specifically with respect to immigrant rights and the lives and learning of transnational families, an ongoing professional and personal interest. It was at an event hosted by one grassroots organization at a Catholic parish that we met leaders from Philadelphia's Indonesian community who invited us to develop a university-community partnership, which would eventually include families from the Parish's Vietnamese, Latine, and Concerned Black Catholic communities as well. Thus began an ongoing labor of love and solidarity that has spanned over a decade and continues as we write these words.

Our CBRE Partnership

Our focus on CBRE later in our careers reflected a shift in orientation rather than a hard paradigmatic turn. We continued to ask many of the same questions, but from a different location and with a new set of collaborators. Since its inception, our project has sought to better understand the ways that immigrant youth and families advocate for themselves in the face of educational inequity (Campano, Ghiso, & Welch, 2016). We have cultivated a shared inquiry where university-based researchers and community members who are involved with a multiethnic and multilingual parish and an immigrant rights coalition come together to investigate and act on a range of educational issues. The CARE Initiative focuses on expanding communities' "right to research" (Appadurai, 2006) the schooling arrangements that impact their experiences and opportunities. Families, K-12 children and youth, and community leaders with diverse backgrounds have been working together to examine the material conditions of schools, to engage in culturally responsive and critical literacy inquiries, and to be in dialogue with educators about how schools need to transform. It has consisted of nested inquiries that have evolved and changed in response to community priorities. Youth and families have researched, among other topics, the high school and college admissions processes, how language barriers and the inappropriate policing of immigration status prevent parental involvement in children's education, racism in the curriculum, and unequal distribution of access to advanced placement courses.

Throughout the years, the CARE Initiative has crafted an intellectual legacy built on the collective knowledge of its members. The interracial, multilingual, and intergenerational nature of the CARE Initiative has made it possible to learn from one another's experiences and to analyze educational obstacles and opportunities from multiple perspectives. There is a wide range in our researchers' ages (elders, parents, community leaders, youth 5–22 years old) and they come together intergenerationally to support each other in their individual life paths and educational trajectories. The families in the partnership speak multiple languages and reflect a range of cultural, ideological, and even political perspectives. Several individuals, for example, were staunchly anti-communist, having fled authoritarian Marxist regimes; others were from minoritized communities in their home countries that had been "red-tagged" and persecuted by right-wing dictators. Many of the participants are involved in their faith-based organizations. A good number have been involved in activism. All the families have experienced racism and economic precarity here in the United States. All have rallied around the superordinate goal of providing their children, and future generations, access to a high-quality education, in Philadelphia and beyond. On the university-side of the partnership, the CARE members, mostly graduate students, have been Latine, European-American, Black, Asian, Native American, and mixed-race. They have grown up Catholic, Jewish, Muslim, and agnostic, come from a range of socioeconomic backgrounds, and several have self-identified as queer. All were educators before entering graduate school.

At this point several of the ostensible paradoxes of our iteration of CBRE may be becoming clear. As educational researchers we critique the education system, including its colonial and white supremacist roots, and how it serves as a mechanism of social reproduction. At the same time, in line with the families in our project, we still harbor faith that schools may be one means for individual and collective self-empowerment and are dedicated to making it better. There are radical educational movements which are forging a world outside of schooling as usual because the system is perhaps beyond repair. We are inspired and challenged by these movements and hope to continue to learn from them, which have a long legacy that harkens back to the Black Panther Liberation Schools, the Freedom Schools, and schools organized around indigenous epistemologies and language revitalization. There are also contradictions in the community, including the fact that this work germinated in a Catholic parish. We ourselves self-identify as garden-variety internally conflicted social justice Catholics; however, we did not partner with the Parish for religious reasons but because it is a site of congregation for diverse Philadelphia families, and the CARE Initiative has always welcomed anyone to become involved who has the passion to participate. While the Catholic

Church has been an instrument of imperialism and continued gender oppression, it has also been "occupied" by community members as a sanctuary and place of resistance to state violence, such as the threat of detention and deportation. We also suspect that there are few community education efforts uninfluenced by legacies of colonialism.

We understand our own CBRE project to be a complement to the public school system, which we still believe remains a necessary, although endangered, pillar of any hope for a genuinely pluralistic democracy. In this way, CBRE can occupy what Kris Gutiérrez (2008) conceptualizes as an interactionally constructed "collective third space" which merges students' own cultural, intellectual, and activist legacies with their educational experiences and aspirations. CBRE can also play an important role in the civic sphere helping to advance what we call epistemic rights, a form of contributive and participatory justice. For example, as we write this, the families in the CARE Initiative are in the process of sharing their research with school educators through presentations, workshops, and inquiry sessions as well as providing testimony to the school district to impact larger policies like budget allocations. We hope this book may be useful to anyone involved in community-based projects which are dedicated to amplifying the voices and knowledge of those who are typically left out of decisions of policy and practice.

While our work alongside families has been central to our understanding of CBRE, we have also been edified intellectually by several other collaborations. Our initial years in the CARE Initiative coincided with each of us working with an increasing number of graduate students, one of the privileges of being employed by well-heeled institutions. Mentoring students has been a passion in both of our lives. Doctoral students we have worked with have had prior lives as teachers, organizers, artists, and school leaders. They, too, came to graduate school to deepen their understanding of and commitment to educational justice, not to leave their previous identities behind to assume a spectatorial academic posture. In fact, if anything, they have expressed that their biggest hesitation about graduate studies is the risk of becoming disconnected from day-to-day, on-the-ground struggles, whether in schools or their communities. Being involved in CBRE has enabled them to bring their fuller selves into their scholarship and, to some degree, remain involved in the types of collective teaching and learning projects that ignited their interest in educational justice in the first place.

The graduate students we have worked with have been invaluable to the CARE Initiative; we would not have been able to sustain the work without them. CBRE involves intensive intellectual and relational labor. More advanced students, as well as elders from the community, have mentored newer generations in our research team. Every incoming student, in turn, has brought their own talents, energy, and perspectives to the work. Our own understanding of CBRE has been forged in dialogue with graduate students and our broader research collective through weekly meetings, community events, academic conferences, coursework, co-authorship, and dissertation supervising. Two inquiries at the heart of our mentoring, and which have fueled the topics in this book, are the following: How can university students be involved in a shared community-based project while simultaneously cultivating their own scholarly interests? And how can they begin to develop the skills and dispositions necessary for forging meaningful partnerships in their dissertation research and in their academic careers? One of our greatest professional rewards has been to witness the innovative ways our current and former students have reimagined and, importantly, enacted careful, ethical, and transformative research alongside others. Our book is in part written with early-career scholars in mind, who may have to make methodological arguments (in proposals or promotion and tenure statements, for example) justifying their interest in collaborative approaches to research in an academy which lionizes a notion of individual genius and productivity.

Goals of This Book

This book explores how educational justice can be conceived through collaborative methodologies that bring together people across institutions and social locations to work towards change. We draw on our long-term partnership as an example to help flesh out the epistemological commitments and possible day-to-day practices of CBRE, and to grapple with the complexities and dilemmas of undertaking educational research driven by community concerns.

   We are not forwarding an orthodox version of CBRE. Each community-based research project in education is different. Our own idiosyncratic journey into this work reveals that the affordances, and limitations, of CBRE are a function of the creative will and intellectual synergy of everyone involved. It is a rhizomatic collaborative endeavor (Larson & Moses, 2015) negotiated within specific contexts rather than a linear set of methods to be applied universally. Thus, we take an inquiry stance into the practices and possibilities of CBRE, which Cochran-Smith and Lytle (2009) describe as "a worldview, a critical habit of mind" dedicated to framing teaching, learning, and research "within webs of social historical, cultural, and political significance" (p. 120). Rather than being prescriptive, we raise methodological questions that may be relevant to all approaches to educational research, such as:

- What research processes and practices can foreground epistemic collaboration?
- How do research foci and questions form and evolve in response to community priorities?
- How might various collaborative arrangements and methods be oriented towards community members' goals for educational justice?
- How can practices of data collection, analysis, and dissemination of findings be grounded in community legacies of activism and resistance?

- How might we navigate the ideological tensions and challenges of this work?
- How do power dynamics figure into every stage of the research process?

Overview of Chapters

Each of the chapters of the book is organized around inquiry questions related to community-based research. We spotlight examples from our partnership to illustrate how the ideas we are discussing might play out in concrete research scenarios and how CBRE can help create the conditions for collaborative inquiry and action on issues of educational (in)justice that are salient to community partners. We view the vignettes and data examples that we feature throughout the book as a platform for inquiry into CBRE rather than a blueprint for others to emulate. The goal is to bring to life the practice of partnering towards a vision of educational change, and how to navigate the complexities, contradictions, and opportunities along the way. The chapters end with questions for reflection, inviting readers to think with the ideas in relationship to their own contexts of research and partnership.

Chapter 2 delineates the foundational principles of community-based research in educational contexts. We characterize CBRE as a conceptual and methodological approach that may encompass a range of research methods, but that is distinguished by its commitment to cultivating partnerships, foregrounding community priorities for educational change, and democratizing knowledge production. These priorities are encapsulated in the idea of advancing epistemic rights. We begin with one of our core principles of valuing community members as intellectuals who are uniquely situated to generate knowledge about educational justice through inquiries into their own lived experiences. We suggest that CBRE has multifarious intellectual and activist roots and ought to be attentive to local legacies. We trace the lineages of CBRE in our own work to the practitioner research movement in education, participatory action research, and critical theories of identity. These approaches value epistemic cooperation across a range of institutional and social locations. They also shed light on the hierarchies inherent in research and practice. Our aim is that readers think expansively about the traditions and subaltern intellectual genealogies that may inform their own CBRE endeavors, and the role these legacies play in helping to create alternative scholarly social formations.

Chapter 3 explores what it means to partner with communities. CBRE projects take time, and their success may not be easily measured by conventional metrics. What would motivate researchers to engage in this relational and labor-intensive form of research? Should they even try to do so? How do university-researchers sit comfortably with the idea of "slow research" (Mountz et al., 2015), especially in institutional contexts which require evidence of productivity? In this chapter, we interrogate our own personal investments in CBRE. We have spent much of our careers mentoring doctoral students to become experts in helping democratize expertise. We highlight three former doctoral students who were involved in the CARE Initiative and their stories about how and why they became interested in community-based research. Their stories illustrate three scholarly virtues that we have found essential for CBRE: critical empathy, epistemic pluralism, and solidarity. We invite readers to reflect on their own desires and motivations to engage in CBRE in the specific contexts of research and practice to which they gravitate.

What are our ethical obligations to others in CBRE? Chapter 4 begins with a critical incident Gerald experienced early in his career when interviewing his grandfather which underscores how research is always carried out in relational contexts. We then address the root problem and concern families have expressed with partnership work, whether with universities, nonprofit organizations, or politicians: that their knowledge and stories are often taken without input from the community or sense of how the partnership may benefit the community. We challenge the presumed neutrality of traditional research paradigms, including their underlying extractivist epistemologies which treat community members as objects to be mined and analyzed rather than subjects who themselves theorize their social worlds. The influence of these dominant research paradigms has prompted us to be explicit about the ethical and professional norms which guide our work and intentional about trying to create more non-hierarchical intellectual relationships. In CBRE, we recognize that all researchers, including university-based ones, are immersed in a flux of rhizomatic relationships which propels the research. Following scholars such as hooks (2000) and Freire (1970), we argue that CBRE might be considered a practice of love, because it is love which holds the promise to break down subject-object dichotomies as we aspire for a research community built on radical belonging and equality.

In Chapter 5, we consider how the co-construction and democratization of knowledge—which can appear both abstract and daunting—might be enacted through regular interactions and project routines. How might the collaborative research be structured and cultivated over time? We provide artifacts and share interactions from several CARE Initiative planning meetings to illustrate how CBRE is a recursive and iterative process of emergent design which involves consensus building at every stage of the research process. CBRE is thus pedagogical. It requires creating spaces for mutual learning and collective decision-making as to the nature and direction of the research. In the CARE Initiative we have drawn on many of our own experiences as teachers as well as community members' skills as organizers in our efforts to orient multiple perspectives toward common research goals. One of the most delicate aspects of CBRE involves being attentive to power dynamics as the research community navigates contesting ideas with care and mutual generosity. At the end of the chapter, we marquee a dialogue between elders in the CARE Initiative and a school leader to demonstrate how consensus can respectfully be built in real-time and in a manner that does not suppress difference and conflict, but works through them in a spirit of solidarity.

In Chapter 6 we discuss collective research design and address how methods of data collection and analysis can be systematic and robust without upholding narrow images of individual scholarly detachment. In CBRE, research instruments and processes are considered ideological, and themselves are subject to ongoing scrutiny and refinement. Within this framework, we think through practices of data collection and analysis to make methods more aligned with the orientation of CBRE. We also reflect on the idea of proprietorship in research and how CBRE often entails multiple inquiries and data sources that different members of the community may draw from for their respective yet interrelated projects.

Chapter 7 addresses how community-based researchers may share their work in creative, transparent, and impactful ways. One imperative of CBRE is to provide opportunities for community members to go public with their work—thus helping to make the research contributions of students, families, educators, and community leaders available to multiple audiences. We provide several examples of going public, including through the sharing of findings at scholarly conferences, publishing in academic journals, making of a participatory documentary and collaborative book project, and engaging school leaders and neighborhood organizations. We argue that research dissemination in CBRE is about much more than the "inclusion" of participant "voices." It is about advancing a more substantial vision of participatory justice which involves, among other considerations, expanding the formats, audiences, and conditions of sharing research so as to value everyone's intellectual contributions and ensure that those who have been historically excluded from decisions of educational research, policy, and practice are well positioned to make an impact.

In Chapter 8, we consider the idea of impact and discuss the potential for CBRE to make a difference in a range of contexts, starting with the partners and co-researchers themselves. CBRE ought to be, first and foremost, a vehicle for individual and collective self-determination. It therefore should be evaluated not by the metrics of those in power, but by the values and aspirations of the community. Some of the impacts of CBRE may be immediate; other times the impact may come to fruition over time. For example, in our own project, we believe one form of impact has been to the research collective itself, in the form of ever-expanding networks of care and belonging and an intergenerational, intellectual commons upon which to build new cycles of inquiry and action. CBRE may also be shaped by and contribute to larger movements for social justice.

Our concluding Chapter 9 offers testimonials from community members about what participating in research has meant to them. We share their words without commentary because they stand on their own.

Overall, this book has been written with several aims in mind. It is a methodology book for scholars who are interested in engaging in Community-Based Research in Education, but we believe that anyone interested in doing research with people will potentially find the methodological questions it raises useful. The book also documents our own career-long efforts to live in the academy on our terms and consistent with our values and full selves as cultural beings, educators, and individuals. We hope that our colleagues in the field might find in it some inspiration to carve out their own spaces within/ against academia, and that the book might resonate with higher education leaders as they support universities to be responsive to the greater public. As we neared completing this book, it also has become a means of expressing how much we cherish and honor everyone we have had the fortune to work, think, and feel alongside in the CARE Initiative, including youth, elders, community leaders, and our own students and mentors. The contingencies of history and fate have entwined the lives of many individuals with sometimes vastly different experiences and with familial and ancestral roots throughout the globe, and these individuals have made the decision to cooperate to make their shared world more caring and just. We believe that their/our story can provide a model to educators and scholars who believe another educational world is possible.

Questions for Reflection

1. What brings you to collaborative and partnership research?
2. Where is your work located?
3. Who are your institutional and community partners?

Note

1 In this book we use Latine as a gender-inclusive term that avoids the Anglicism of Latinx (see DaSilva Iddings & Rosoff, 2023).

References

Appadurai, A. (2006). The right to research. *Globalization, Societies, and Education*, *4*(2), 167–177.

Bang, M., Faber, L., Gurneau, J., Marin, A., & Soto, C. (2015). Community-based design research: Learning across generations and strategic transformations of institutional relations toward axiological innovations. *Mind, Culture, and Activity*, *23*(1), 28–41.

Campano, G., Ghiso, M. P., & Welch, B. (2016). *Partnering with immigrant communities: Action through literacy*. Teachers College Press.

Coburn, C. E., & Penuel, W. R. (2016). Research–practice partnerships in education: Outcomes, dynamics, and open questions. *Educational Researcher*, *45*, 48–54.

Cochran-Smith, M., & Lytle, S. L. (2009). *Inquiry as stance: Practitioner research for the next generation*. Teachers College Press.

DaSilva Iddings, A. C., & Rosoff, J. (2023). Decolonial praxis and the language and literacy education of Latine immigrant and refugee students. *Language Arts*, *100*(6), 472–483.

Freire, P. (1970). *Pedagogy of the oppressed*. Continuum.

Gutiérrez, K. (2008). Developing a sociocritical literacy in the third space. *Reading Research Quarterly*, *43*(2), 148–164.

hooks, b. (2000). *All about love: New visions*. William Morrow.

Ishimaru. A. M., & Bang, M. (2022). Designing with families for just futures in the Family Leadership Design Collaborative. *Journal of Family Diversity in Education, 4*(2), 130–140.

Larson, J., & Moses, R. (Eds.). (2015). *Community literacies and shared resources for transformation*. Routledge.

Mountz, A., Bonds, A., Mansfield, B., Loyd, J., Hyndman, J., Walton-Roberts, M., Basu, R., Whitson, R., Hawkins, R., Hamilton, T., & Curran, W. (2015). For slow scholarship: A feminist politics of resistance through collective action in the neo-liberal university. *ACME: An International E-Journal for Critical Geographies, 14*(4), 1235–1259.

Nuñez, I. (2021). "Because we have to speak English at school": Transfronterizx children translanguaging identity to cross the academic border. *Research in the Teaching of English, 56*(1), 10–32.

Oliveira, G. (2018). *Motherhood across borders: Immigrants and their children in Mexico and New York*. New York University Press.

Peurach, D. J., Russell, J. L., Chen-Vogel, L, & Penuel, W. R. (Eds.). (2022). *Foundational handbook on improvement-focused educational research*. Rowan & Littlefield.

Rusoja, A. (2022). "Our community is filled with experts": The critical intergenerational literacies of Latinx immigrants that facilitate a communal pedagogy of resistance. *Research in the Teaching of English, 56*(3), 301–327.

2 What Is Community-Based Research in Education?

Belonging and Common Cause

In the spring of 2022, two youth members of the CARE Initiative, Ivy and Lukas,[1] presented at a Zoom event that sought to address the interlocking issues of education and housing justice. The speakers also included residents of an affordable housing complex being targeted for demolition, community activists, and university faculty and students: it was a genuinely polyphonic literacy event, in the Bakhtinian sense (Bakhtin, 1984), bringing together voices and expertise from various social and institutional locations which, in concert, disrupted the seeming inevitability of deeply entrenched inequities that impact local families. It was also just one small action in a whole constellation of events that grew out of the larger movement for Black Lives and the city's rich and ongoing legacies of resistance and liberation.

The panel highlighted the demands of community organizers: that local universities intervene to protect the affordable housing complex, one of the last vestiges of the working-class Black community contiguous to the campus, and that they make Payments In Lieu of Taxes (PILOTs) to the city school district, which is severely underfunded. Universities are some of the largest property owners, continuously expanding and availing themselves of public services, yet most do not contribute property taxes due to their non-profit status, an essential revenue source for public schools. The presenters challenged the "UniverCity" (Baldwin, 2021) of its status as neutral ivory towers, exposing its geopolitical influences on residents. In support of PILOTs, Lukas and Ivy presented their original research on the material conditions of learning in the city school district, including toxic school buildings imbued with asbestos and lead, which had led to yet another round of school shutterings in our city. They also discussed their findings on the unconscionable counselor to student ratios, the lack of school nurses, the tracking system, and the need to shift resources from policing to care in the education system and society writ large. All the speakers drew parallels between housing and education injustices, both of which have involved the dispossession and displacement of predominantly Black, Brown, and immigrant families. They pooled their respective expertise to gain a deeper understanding of the inequalities of our

DOI: 10.4324/9781003279686-2

city and, in the process, prefigured new social arrangements premised on collective liberation.

If you turned back the clock eleven years earlier, to the beginning of the CARE Initiative, it may have been hard to imagine Ivy and Lukas, then in kindergarten and first grade, sharing their empirical findings to an audience of close to two hundred local activists and university faculty and students— presentations which were, by all accounts, informative, persuasive, and poignant. As young children, their first activity in our partnership was a pen pal exchange with Masters students from Gerald's literacy course and the Indonesian community's Sunday School, where they honed their reading and writing skills and the university students could examine examples of early literacy. This idea of the letter exchange was initiated and organized by Ivy's mother, an incredible neighborhood and parish leader. Although we were not engaging in official research yet at that point, we were in the process of developing a trusting and reciprocally beneficial relationship between the university team and families from the South Philadelphia immigrant community. We were laying the foundation for a long-term partnership.

In retrospect, therefore, Ivy's and Lukas' scholarly community engagement is not surprising. Over the past decade, with the support of graduate students and elders, they have been conducting research on topics that impact them and their communities, including immigration rights, health care, environmental justice, civic engagement, and educational access. They have attended numerous scholarly conferences and have even published in academic journals, including venues dedicated to the work of youth researchers (e.g., Gultom et al., 2019). These experiences have helped them demystify academia but also, because of the culturally relevant nature of the research, make academia their own: a means through which they can deepen their understanding of themselves and their relationship to the world. For Lukas and Ivy and their peers in the CARE Initiative, involvement in CBRE has contributed to success in school and beyond. For example, all the youth in our project to date have graduated high school and the majority have gained access to institutions of higher education, although several have chosen other valuable life paths or have paused their post-secondary studies because of financial obstacles.

These potential impacts of the CARE Initiative are ideally consonant with the desires of the families in our partnership, many of whom see education as one potential vehicle for greater life-opportunities and a source of hope. We want everyone involved in our project to thrive, on their own terms. For some, this means gaining access to the opportunities that we ourselves have had as university-based researchers; for others, it means involvement in intellectual and activist groups outside of schooling. All the members of the research community move across ostensibly disparate social spaces and nurture multiple aspirations and dimensions of their identities.

In our research partnership, individual and collective wellbeing are ineluctably entwined. In the process of gaining valuable academic skills and experiences, Lukas and Ivy were also part of collaborative knowledge projects geared towards systemic change and transformation. Over the years they have worked alongside others to contribute to our shared understanding of the education system and how to make it more universally uplifting and empowering. This valuing of epistemic cooperation and coalition, in the service of education justice, is at the heart of our understanding of CBRE.

We define Community-Based Research in Education (CBRE) as long-term research collaborations with families, leaders, and educators as they investigate issues of educational access and equity that impact their communities. CBRE shares a family resemblance with other collaborative approaches to educational research, including Participatory Action Research (PAR), Youth Participatory Action Research (YPAR), Research-Practice Partnerships (RPPs), Participatory Ethnography, and Communities of Inquiry. What is essential to CBRE is that it derives from the interests and questions of community members, has a commitment to sustained collaboration over time, and seeks to advance what we call epistemic rights in the service of educational justice. We understand epistemic rights as ensuring the conditions for people to have the material support and time to inquire into the inequities of the world, including of the education system, and how to make it better. Epistemic rights involve (but are not limited to): the right to have one's own knowledge and interests taken seriously; to be able to participate in multiple, collective knowledge projects both within and outside educational institutions; to have access to various approaches to inquiry; to be exposed to resources and networks that may expand one's own epistemic horizons; to cultivate intellectual self-assurance; to go public with research to a range of audiences; and to be able to take action on what one knows. It is the right to construct knowledge in the service of a more just world.

CBRE has a flexible organizational structure that accommodates both contingency and possibility. Because CBRE entails an intellectual and creative alchemy by all members of a research team, forged through relationships, its specific forms of inquiry may evolve over time, or it may involve multiple approaches. For example, at the beginning of our own CBRE initiative, we were asking some fundamental ethnographic questions, including the following:

- What are the patterns of educational inequity in the youth's schooling?
- What are the aspirations of community members?
- How do they understand the role of education in their lives?
- What work is already going on in the community to support educational justice?
- What are the most salient issues of power and hierarchy?
- How do youth and families' immigrant experiences and racialized identities intersect with schooling in the United States?

This ethnographic backdrop assisted us in better understanding the context and seeing how our interests and experiences could meaningfully intersect with community goals for educational justice. As our collaboration progressed, we partnered with youth and adults to jointly design and carry out research, as well as conceptualize our group's practices of partnering. Throughout, we have engaged together in a community of inquiry, thinking alongside one another around issues of educational equity and access. Families have conducted interviews, surveys, archival research, photovoice, content and discourse analysis, participant observation, and more in the service of their research. CBRE embraces a robust pluralism with respect to research methods, and the methods unitized will invariably be informed by the talents and expertise of those involved.

There are at least three interrelated themes in CBRE: explicit attention to what constitutes "community" and its role in research; a commitment to democratizing knowledge production; and a sustained effort to work collectively across institutional and social boundaries. These principles will invariably look different as actualized within specific research collectivities, animated by their intellectual histories, disciplinary focus, context, and sociopolitical realities.

What Does "Community" Signal in CBRE?

One salient methodological feature of CBRE is a recognition of the emplaced nature of inquiry. The word "community" in CBRE signals self-reflexivity about the situated dimensions of research. As scholars from Latin American subaltern studies have stated, in a subversive play on Descartes' famous *cogito, ergo sum*, "we are where we think" (Mignolo, 2011). The geopolitics of knowledge production operates on a world-wide scale, such as between the global north and the global south. But it also is evident on a more fine-grained level, such as between neighborhoods in the same city, even blocks, and various social formations sometimes occupying the same geographic spaces, especially in contexts of stark inequality.

We recognize, in the tradition of ethnography, that communities are not homogenous and stable, but are internally diverse and actively made and (re) negotiated. The boundaries of who is or is not part of a community, how those boundaries are reinforced and contested, and who is positioned to "represent" a community need to be grappled with in any research collaboration. The goal of CBRE for university-based researchers, however, is not to become an "expert" on any community. We are aware and wary of ethnography's colonial history of classifying and categorizing people. We want to respect everyone's "right to opacity" (Glissant, 1997). The goal is rather to work in intellectual solidarity alongside community members. We encourage those interested in CBRE to become aware of the complex social and political landscape of any context they hope to work in so as to navigate its dynamics thoughtfully and ethically. As we will discuss further in this section, "community members" are also thinking, conducting inquiry, and theorizing from their respective social and geopolitical locations, from what feminists of color characterize as the "physical realities of [their] lives" (Moraga & Anzaldúa, 1983, p. 23) and from the (trans)local intellectual and activist legacies to which they are heir.

In research partnerships, there are often numerous communities, including the fact that members of the university-based research team constitute an intellectual community themselves. For example, in our own project, as university faculty, we have regular meetings with students who have developed relationships with us over time through coursework and mentoring. Our institutional affiliations may provide us with scholarly training and access to resources, but it by no means offers an unbiased point from which to conduct inquiry. We are mindful that we engage in research from a very specific location ourselves.

The university is a major presence in many cities, and there is no question they do much good in the world. At their best, universities are bastions of academic freedom, cutting-edge research, and critical inquiry. They remain one of the few public spheres where productive debate, deliberation and dissent are nurtured, a cornerstone for a genuinely democratic society. But they are also sites of social and political contestation. Many scholars and students, learning from community activists, have turned their critical gaze onto institutions of higher learning to interrogate, for example, their complicity with human enslavement, settler colonialism, the prison industrial complex, gentrification, and exploitive research agendas. They are demanding that local universities reckon with these ongoing histories of oppression. Calls to decolonize the university, of course, raise a larger set of questions regarding if, how, and to what degree institutions of higher education are willing to engage competing understandings of their histories, missions, and obligations to the public. We are living through another period where the autonomy of higher education is under assault by outside political and corporate forces. We both critique the university's complicity with these forces and staunchly defend its highest ideals. CBRE, we believe, may play a small part in fortifying the university's teaching and research mission and enhancing democratic engagement for a multiracial democracy. We strive to work within our own institutions, drawing inspiration from what Harney and Moten (2013) refer to as its "undercommons," participating in new intellectual communities that do not conform to alienating disciplinary or professional edicts. At the same time, we are also aware that there are limits to how radical our work can be when "we are thinking" from universities which are torn between their teaching/research missions and their corporate administrative logics.

We have cast the relationship between universities and their surrounding communities in binary terms, and for good reason. Universities are often exclusionary and characterized by concentrated wealth and privilege. At the same time, when considering individuals, the boundaries may be more porous than they initially appear. For example, most of the members on the university-side of the research team in our own project have shared affinities with community members based on their own racialized or class-based experiences, backgrounds as immigrants, and/or political commitments.

A number of us also self-identify as academic workers and see ourselves in solidarity with other workers throughout the city. And, conversely, many of the community members may have different degrees of relationships with local universities and colleges, and—we have found—significant affective investments in higher education, especially for future generations. One of the aims of CBRE is to help mediate a greater, and more reciprocal, flow of movement—of people, ideas, resources, and carework—between the university and its surrounding neighborhoods.

As university-based scholars, we try to be innovative about how we can repurpose and mobilize the resources of the university toward community ends. Some examples which we highlight in this book include the following: using university conferences and classes as a platform for community members to share their scholarship; supporting first generation university students who desire to work in solidarity with the community to apply for compensated research fellowship opportunities; creating courses that have a community engaged component; having the youth use the film studio of the university for their own documentary project; recruiting education Masters students to support youth and families with their academic needs; and generally "occupying" the space of the university to avail ourselves of its amenities (rooms, libraries, computers, maker spaces, etc.) for both scholarly projects and social gatherings. However, there is so much more that can be done to create bridges between the university and communities and support the epistemic rights of families and youth. We believe it only benefits universities to have a thriving public presence on their campuses and more trusting and reciprocal relations with their surrounding neighborhoods.

Democratizing Knowledge Production: (Some) Lineages of CBRE

Is there a way of being intellectual that isn't social? When I think about the way we use the term "study," I think we are committed to the idea that study is what you do with other people. It's talking and walking around with other people, working, dancing, suffering, some irreducible convergence of all three, held under the name of speculative practice. The notion of a rehearsal—being in a kind of workshop, playing in a band, in a jam session, or old men sitting on a porch, or people working together in a factory—there are these various modes of activity. The point of calling it "study" is to mark that the incessant and irreversible intellectuality of these activities is already present. These activities aren't ennobled by the fact that we now say, "oh, if you did these things in a certain way, you could be said to have been studying." To do these things is to be involved in a kind of common intellectual practice. What's important is to recognize that that has been the case—because that recognition allows you to access a whole, varied, alternative history of thought.

(Harney & Moten, 2013, p. 110)

CBRE methodology is about universalizing the role of the intellectual. The extended quote by Fred Moten underscores that knowledge generation through systematic inquiry—what we might call research—is not solely the purview of academics but happens on the ground by everyday people who together are seeking to solve problems that impact their lives. Moten discusses how the naming of these social inquiries as "study" marks these activities as a "common intellectual practice" that is always already present in communities. Thus, while there are academic lineages of research seeking to address educational inequities (some of which, it can be argued, reproduce such inequities), there are also community-based efforts to research, reform, and reimagine education: "a whole, varied, alternative history of thought" derived from intellectual genealogies that may have been buried in dominant accounts of schooling and improvement. CBRE seeks to be attentive to the legacies of activism and critical work that already exist in communities and every individual's fundamental capacity to inquire into and theorize their realities.

Within academia, Community-Based Research draws from several intellectual traditions, such as Freirean popular education and participatory research (Strand et al., 2003), and has been employed across fields to refer to a range of research partnerships that expand participation and act on social injustices (Stoecker, 2009). Community-Based Research "insists on the democratization and demystification of knowledge as it challenges some basic assumptions about knowledge itself: what constitutes valid knowledge, how it is best produced (and by whom), and who should control it" (Strand et al., 2003, p. 7). Much current work under the umbrella of "Community-Based Research" is focused on the health fields. Vera Caine and Judy Mills (2016), for example, forward considerations for community-based research design by drawing from several projects on HIV awareness and prevention undertaken alongside indigenous communities in Canada. Our work shares a similar commitment to working alongside communities, but is also different, in part because of the methods used (qualitative and participatory approaches rather than randomized trials or quantitative methods), the range of stakeholders involved (school districts, educational leaders, activist groups, children and youth, and families), and our own focus on educational access and equity.

Within the field of education, Larson and Moses (2015) discuss a community-based partnership which links the University of Rochester with the Beechwood neighborhood in Rochester, NY. The different "hubs" of research in the partnership encompass schools as well as other community-led social justice efforts, such as the transformation of a corner store into a Freedom Market. Larson and Moses (2015) highlight how educational justice is part of long-standing research relationships that cut across various projects such that: (1) educational "improvement" becomes framed by broader understandings of inequality that influence school dynamics, student learning, and family wellbeing; and (2) the teaching and learning that happens in community spaces becomes visible. In a similar vein, Marciano and colleagues (Marciano et al., 2020) discuss how in The Youth Voices Project—an ongoing, multi-year participatory research initiative within a subsidized housing community in the US Midwest—youth examined educational systems as well as make issues of equity central to their inquiries outside of schools. Given the increased attention to research partnerships in educational contexts (Penuel & Gallagher, 2017), we believe it is helpful to articulate the specificities of what we call Community-Based Research in Education (CBRE).

Our conceptualization of CBRE is informed by critical theories and methodologies with a focus on how they have been taken up in the field of education. Such scholarship interrogates how power operates through the institution of schooling and the relationship between knowledge, action, and social transformation. We offer the genealogical sketches below as one starting point for tracing the commitments and practices central to our own understanding of CBRE, but other projects will no doubt have other influences that have informed their own thinking and practices.

Critical Theories of Identity and Their Role in Education

CBRE understands education—and educational (in)equity—as produced through institutional and social systems. From this perspective, teaching and learning are always political and require an analysis of power. As Freire (1970) articulated, schools can perpetuate inequality through a banking model that views learners as passive subjects and often reproduce entrenched hierarchies along class and other markers of difference; conversely, pedagogy can also be a vehicle for social transformation. A critical perspective on educational inequality and justice thus challenges initiatives aimed at "improvement" that are based on deficit assumptions of learners. Rather, the attention shifts to destabilizing the presumed neutrality of schooling to make visible how the unequal distribution of power and resources positions students from minoritized backgrounds as failing, thus inflicting symbolic and literal violence (Love, 2023; Patel, 2013). Curricula, practices, and policies that construct learners as "at risk" and a subsequent public discourse of educational crisis (Vasudevan & Campano, 2009) work against understanding the array of sociocultural factors that influence youth's learning both in and out of school. This includes their community cultural wealth (Yosso, 2005) and familial repertoires of educational knowledge and advocacy (de los Ríos & Molina, 2020; Oliveira, 2018). For example, Baker-Bell (2020) has dissected how Anti-Black linguistic racism in schools perpetuates "violence, persecution, dehumanization, and marginalization of Black language speakers" (p. 7) and has developed antiracist scholarship by drawing on community legacies of freedom.

There are many intellectual traditions that partnerships may draw on to interrogate the relationship between educational (in)justice and systems of power. For instance, theories of coloniality help us see how schools have been imperial tools of subjugation, cultural genocide, and dispossession (e.g., Campano et al., 2021; Rodríguez et al., 2021). Decolonial scholars and thinkers in the Black and Chicanx feminist traditions, among others, point to the ways that communities of color have collectively agitated for social transformation, with educational justice as part of a broader social movement of liberation (e.g., de los Ríos et al., 2019; Sealey-Ruiz, 2021; Strong et al., 2023).

Our partnership has been grounded in feminist of color theories of identity, inquiry, and resistance (Alcoff, 2006; Anzaldúa, 1999; Lorde, 1984; Moya, 2002). These conceptual frames understand identity as socially mediated, yet also referencing real social phenomena and matrices of power which perpetuate inequality. As Chicana scholar Paula Moya (2011) argues, "paying special attention to the struggles for social justice of people with subordinated identities is especially crucial to the process of investigating the functioning of a hierarchical social order" (p. 85) and "central to our collective ability to create coalition across difference" (p. 85). In the CARE Initiative, members of the research partnership have mobilized their respective personal experiences being involved in grass-roots social struggles against oppression to investigate the systemic barriers to educational access and strategize how to work together to dismantle them. They draw on the epistemic privilege (Campano, 2007; Moya, 2002) derived from their racialized identities to both discern and break patterns of educational inequality.

Participatory and Action-Oriented Approaches

The methodological lineages which inform our own understanding of CBRE include participatory action research with adults and youth (e.g., Cammarota & Fine, 2008; Caraballo et al., 2017). Fine (2008) describes PAR as "a radical *epistemological challenge* to the traditions of social science" because, as she notes,

> Participatory action researchers ground our work in the recognition that expertise and knowledge are widely distributed. PAR further assumes that those who have been *most* systematically excluded, oppressed, or denied carry specifically revealing wisdom about the history, structure, consequences, and the fracture points in unjust social arrangements. PAR embodies a democratic commitment to break the monopoly on who holds knowledge and for whom social research should be undertaken.
>
> (p. 215)

Participatory research thus challenges "the normative production of knowledge" (Cahill, 2007, p. 326), seeking to disrupt existing asymmetries between the "researcher" and the "researched" and instead fostering equitable collaborations between university-based scholars and educators, youth, and families. Central to this scholarship is the recognition that those marginalized by oppressive schooling systems—students and youth—ought to be at the forefront of bringing about change (e.g., Mirra, Garcia & Morrell, 2015). Participatory research often draws on critical feminist (Lorde, 1984), decolonial (Mignolo, 2000), indigenous (Smith, 2021), critical race (Cammarota & Fine, 2008) and other theoretical lenses which understands subaltern ways of knowing and being as "epistemic goods" central to social transformation (Campano et al., 2020, p. 225).

Participatory research assumes a critical stance towards schooling and views socially just action as an overarching aim of the inquiry process. Caraballo and Lyiscott (2020) note how these approaches gained traction during the 1980s and 1990s as some researchers concluded that "positivist and postpositivist assumptions did not serve marginalized individuals and communities" (p. 195). Participatory research is often guided, accordingly, by either explicit or implicit realist epistemologies and a desire to revolutionize the nature and purposes of inquiry. PAR is predicated on "assuming active and full participation in the research process" (Morrell, 2008, p. 158) by all stakeholders. In education, such stakeholders include "student researchers as well as push outs, educators, [and] university professors" (Cammarota & Fine, 2008, p. 5). In Youth Participatory Action Research, the emphasis is specifically on engaging youth and learning from and alongside them as one core constituency who "do[es] not often participate as researchers or experts in dialogues concerning the present and future of urban education" (Morrell, 2008, p. 156).

There is a rich tradition in educational research on using participatory methods as a means of addressing the structural inequalities that impact communities of color. Cahill (2007), for example, explores the transformative dimensions of participatory research by characterizing their explicit "commitment to creating conditions for social change" (p. 362). Drawing on a YPAR project through which undocumented Latine youth in Salt Lake City examined inequities in higher education, Cahill describes how youth researchers investigated the oppressions confronting their own communities. Along similar lines, Fine (2018) describes a range of participatory action research projects which, while unique, are unified by a shared need to "trouble the common sense about unjust arrangements that seem so natural or deserved" (p. 6). Though emanating from the particulars of different contexts, the scholarship documenting PAR and YPAR provides evidence of endeavors that center historically marginalized voices "to address the asymmetries of an unjust world" (Cahill, 2007, p. 366) and to reconsider for whom and by whom research is conducted.

Practitioner Inquiry

One methodological tradition of democratizing knowledge production that has informed our conceptions of CBRE is the practitioner research movement. Emerging in the late 1980s and related to participatory and action-oriented approaches, teacher/practitioner research seeks to "challenge the hegemony of an exclusively university-generated knowledge base for teaching" (Cochran-Smith & Lytle, 1999, p. 16). Assuming a democratic approach to inquiry, practitioner research is conducted with the assumption that knowledge about educational problems and solutions can be generated within educational sites themselves. Like community-based research, then, it also upends the notion that knowledge about practice flows unidirectionally from formal institutions—such as universities, think tanks, and corporations—into contexts of teaching and learning. What counts as a site of practice is also expansively conceived: while examples abound of teacher researchers theorizing from their classrooms, others have also taken up the methodology out-of-school contexts. For example, Rusoja (2017) utilized practitioner inquiry to explore intergenerational pedagogies of resistance within a grass-roots Latine immigrant rights organization.

Across practitioner research literature and within our own project, several aspects of this methodology have proven vital. Assuming an inquiry stance in practitioner research entails continuous reflection, for example, about the power dynamics inherent within sites of practice as well as the ways in which practitioners themselves are helping or hindering the cause of social justice. Central to an inquiry stance and the practitioner research movement is seeing teaching as political and as a "professional practice with the capacity for and the commitment to improving itself" (Lytle, 2008, p. 373).

Another dimension of practitioner research is the importance of pursuing knowledge within multi-perspectival communities of inquiry. This has been central to our own work, as the members of our partnership bring a range of histories, identities, and perspectives to bear on the inquiry process. Cochran-Smith and Lytle (2009) argue that communities of inquiry take an inquiry stance on practice involve more than concerns about the instrumental aspects of teaching ("how to get things done") but also questioning the social and political assumptions underlying educational practices, especially those that are taken-for-granted or may seem routine, with an eye towards equity. According to Cochran-Smith and Lytle, this entails

> a continual process of making current arrangements problematic, questioning the ways knowledge and practice are constructed, evaluated, and used; and assuming that part of the work of practitioners individually and collectively is to participate in educational and social change.
>
> (p. 121)

From this methodological vantage point, knowledge is generated through concerted inquiries of those involved in the daily material work of education. Importantly, practitioner research has taken root outside of school district efforts to "train" teachers, organized by teacher groups themselves to improve learning opportunities for students and schooling conditions. The legacies of the practitioner research movement of "blurring the boundaries of research and practice" and "conceptualizing practice as a critical and theory-building process" (Cochran-Smith & Lytle, 1999, p. 18) are important considerations for CBRE, positioning educators as creators of knowledge and re-defining practice as a theoretical.

Epistemic Rights in Research Partnerships

The lineages we've described emphasize several tenets we find germane to CBRE: that contexts of educational practice are rich sites for theorizing about educational equity; that those most impacted by on the-ground inequities— such as educators, families, and youths—have an epistemic advantage in inquiring into injustice and how we might advance efforts for change; and that research oriented toward social transformation is best accomplished in and through collectivities. As Mohanty (2018) argues, the knowledge derived from minoritized social locations is a product of deliberate grass-roots inquiry about the systems of power and social relationships that structure our world. Mohanty (2018) notes,

> Conscious social organizing is a form of reflection, often a form of sustained theoretical reflection. And the capacity to do such organizing (and the reflection it embodies) is not the unique property of a political or intellectual vanguard group; all of us ordinary mortals draw on this ability as we live our daily social lives, cooperating with others to make sense of things as we engage in our various common projects.
>
> (p. 425)

Following Mohanty, we view everyone as a theorizer, organizer, and intellectual as we cooperate to construct a collaborative process of research directed toward a shared vision of educational justice. We believe that CBRE and universities may play an important role in advancing communities' epistemic rights.

A note might be in order as to why we ground our vision of CBRE in rights discourse. Human rights, including what we call epistemic rights, are the rights that one has by virtue of the dignity of being human, irrespective of the contingencies of historical circumstance, such as national citizenship. Human rights thinking has garnered significant attention across disciplines in large part because of the tension between its idealistic promise as one means to address oppression and how it has often been actualized in the realpolitiks of national and international contexts. Most prominently articulated in the Universal Declaration of Human Rights in 1994, human rights as a social movement committed to a vision of supranational law and justice did not fully flower until the 1970s and perhaps began to wilt somewhat in the 1990s (Moyn, 2012). Nevertheless, its language continues to permeate our "age of rights" and has perhaps evolved to inform a diverse set of (sometimes contradictory) agendas.

There are challenges to embracing human rights, beginning with its "tautological definition"—human rights are the rights of humans—which leaves "no ultimate justification or authority … by which rights are guaranteed" (Parikh & Matlin, 2015, p. 27). As the disability theorist Tobin Siebers (2007) reminds us, human rights "carries with it 18th Century baggage" regarding what qualities constitute a fully realized "human," which has been, from a white supremacist and heteronormative patriarchal perspective, an historically variable category, at times excluding or partially including, for example, the enslaved, women, individuals who identify as LGBTQ+, those who are colonized, who are impoverished, or are disabled. This is why we do not characterize CBRE as a "humanizing methodology," departing from Freire. We cannot humanize those who are already human, and claiming to do so perpetuates a kind of colonizing discourse (as only one example, the Thomasite educators during the era of American Colonization of the Philippines were charged with civilizing America's "little brown brothers" through education, so they could become more—though never fully—"human").

While the appeal of a universal framework is that it may offer a means of adjudicating injustice and inhumane treatment across the globe, many human rights struggles are mired in a fundamental paradox most famously articulated by Hannah Arendt (1976) when she posed "Who has the right to have rights?" For example, what entity protects the rights of those without papers who may be escaping state-sanctioned persecution? Human rights as a transnational framework for social justice is ultimately dependent on states, who are often themselves complicit in human rights violations, to ensure their enforcement.

Given human rights' challenges and troublesome history, why ground CBRE in rights discourse and, specifically, in an idea of epistemic rights? We began to embrace the idea of human rights in our own project because many of the participants from the CARE Initiative have invoked an ideal of universal dignity and claimed a set of rights in the service of "positive freedoms" (Paul, 2023), ones that provide baseline opportunities to support self-determination. These include the right to mobility, to work, to healthcare, to a livable wage, to affordable housing and, importantly for our partnership, the right to a high-quality education, a penultimate goal which all the members of the CARE Initiative share, despite having different racialized, cultural, and minoritized experiences. They have a perception of themselves as human rights holders. Human rights may thus provide a meta-narrative that can support diverse individuals in finding common ground. As Clapham (2015) notes, "human rights were and are increasingly invoked and claimed in contexts of anti-imperialism, anti-apartheid, anti-racism, anti-Semitism, anti-homophobia, anti-islamophobia, and feminist and indigenous struggles everywhere" (p. 23). The concept of human rights has been one mechanism for linking social justice struggles, making visible, for example, how the incarceration of Black youth and the detainment and deportation of immigrant families are part of a similar logic of racial subordination (Rodriguez, 2020), a phenomenon which youth in the CARE Initiative have investigated.

If human rights are to be retained, we believe that they can be reimagined to be radically more inclusive and attentive to issues of power. Scholars, for example, have argued for conceptualizing human rights from the standpoint of our shared vulnerabilities and from an ethos of interdependence. Judith Butler (2004) highlights how precarity in the face of global calamities such as war and climate change ought to remind us of our commonalities and our implication in one another's lives. This shared, although differentially distributed, condition of precarity can become the basis for claiming rights and a grounding for solidarity. From a disability studies perspective, Siebers (2007) identifies the role of bodily fragility as a means of "locat[ing] the activation of human rights at the point of greatest need, requiring the recognition of humanity in those at the greatest risk of losing their place in the world" (p. 19). These characterizations of human rights underscore the connectivity among people and contexts and reinforcing the necessity of coalition building in social justice efforts.

We offer our own understanding of rights not solely as an ideology invoked by the state, but as practices enacted collectively on the ground by organizers, educators, youth, and community members. Fregoso (2014) draws on the Zapatistas to help articulate on alternative decolonial understanding of rights "as existing in their exercise, prior to and irrespective of their legalization" (p. 254). This would mean "bypass[ing] state endorsement" and instead conceiving of rights as "lived and embodied practices" (Fregoso, 2014, p. 594). There are "vernacular" human rights demands produced from on-the-ground social struggles that can "contest and challenge oppressive practices and relations and importantly, generate new visions of justice." (Madhok, 2021, p. 6). These portrayals mirror how human rights are invoked and enacted by members of the CARE Initiative and local organizers in our research context, who at once agitate for change to codified laws and enact a vision of rights in their day-to-day practices in ways that supersede current legislative protections. Rights are not only sanctioned by the state or by international institutions, but most urgently and cogently articulated and claimed from the ground up, through everyday social struggles.

Members of the CARE Initiative navigate multiple, intersecting forms of oppression, including racism, anti-immigrant sentiments and policies, work exploitation, and educational access, and thus find themselves at the nexus of multiple human rights struggles. But we believe that one common denominator underneath them all is what we are calling epistemic rights. People need opportunities to access and generate knowledge of all the issues impacting their lives. Our understanding of epistemic rights is indebted to Appadurai's idea of "the right to research" (2006), which he characterizes as "the capacity to systematically increase the horizons of one's current knowledge, in relation to some task, goal, or aspiration" (p. 176). We highlight "epistemic rights" in addition to the "the right to research" because we believe epistemic practices can take a range of forms that go beyond, but are not mutually exclusive to, conventional academic understandings of research. We embrace an epistemic pluralism that views acting in the world as inseparable from understanding the world.

One question which has been posed to us is how the notion of epistemic rights differs from the right to an education, which ideally should be about gaining access to knowledge for self-empowerment. We are both former teachers, and we do not wish to draw unnecessary distinctions between CBRE and progressive and powerful classroom teaching and learning. In fact, our own understanding of CBRE is informed by traditions of critical pedagogy and inquiry, and it is very much our hope that CBRE can inform schooling. But our commitment to CBRE arose out of the reality that schooling is at once a mechanism for community empowerment as well as for social reproduction and student alienation (e.g. Gadsden & Dixon-Román, 2017; Nasir, 2012). As members of the CARE Initiative themselves have researched, schooling itself often creates an adverse hermeneutical climate for the investigation and interpretation of a students' own personal, familial, and historical experiences and may often exacerbate or perpetuate oppression. Take, for example, the emphasis on the hyper-standardization of the curriculum or high-stakes bell-curve testing, the assaults of what is deemed Critical Race Theory or the banning of books that reflect the genuine diversity of students' identities. By advancing their epistemic rights through CBRE, community members at once critique the education system while simultaneously trying to make it better and, in the tradition of the greatest human rights movements, pushing education to live up to its most universal and edifying ideals.

Creating New Scholarly Communities: Challenges and Possibilities

Ideally, through CBRE, a new community will emerge in the borderlands between institutions and the public. We are inspired by Michael Hames-García's notion that one's "community are those with whom we make common cause" (2011, p. xv). As we showcase in the examples throughout this book, the cause for the CARE Initiative is educational access and justice for all. Engaging in CBRE entails a continual process of working through, in collaboration with others, how to collectively determine the "common cause" in specific contexts of research and practice, and how to navigate the complexities inherent in these efforts.

The cause of educational justice requires coalitional work grounded in community agency and resistance. We define agency simply as the ability of youth and families to discern, within educational contexts, issues of power and inequity and to act in a manner that enhances greater individual and community empowerment. This link between agency and collectivity is indebted to broader social struggles such as the feminist movement and anti-racist activism, and we believe it is also crucial to the field of education. Our understanding of agency thus aims to challenge deeply entrenched notions of the independent agent, who, through an exertion of individual will, effort, and talent, is able to transcend their circumstances and compete academically.

These notions of independence are in the ideological DNA of much of educational policy and research—such as standardization, tracking, high-stakes testing, and measurement—and continually resurface in popular concepts such as "resilience" and "grit" (Campano & Simon, 2010). We acknowledge that individuals do indeed make choices, have responsibilities, and play a role in their own learning; but we also suggest that the atomization of agency obscures both group oppression as well as how inquiry is often an outgrowth of progressive social movements premised on interdependence (Ghiso, 2016; Lorde, 1984). We are indebted, for example, to the idea of feminist consciousness raising groups, where individuals may arrive at more empowering readings of their circumstances through ongoing dialogue with —and activism alongside—others. These collective projects have clear pedagogical affinities with Freire's (1970) concept of conscientização, and realist theories of identity and experience (Mohanty, 1997; Moya, 2002). Drawing on theories of intersectionality developed by Crenshaw (2017) and the Combahee River Collective (2014), Satya Mohanty (2018) discussed how having a multiplicity of experiences and identities—both within oneself and in collectivities—is more than an issue of inclusivity. These experiences are also, importantly, profound epistemic resources.

In disrupting the normative boundaries between academic research and practice and prioritizing coalitions, we believe CBRE is a form of what Olúfẹ́mi Táíwò (2022) describes as a "constructive politics" that "engages directly in the task of redistributing social resources and power" (p. 84). In the realm of "knowledge practices," constructive politics "focuses on institutions and practices of information gathering that are strategically useful or challenging social institutions themselves, not just the symptoms manifest in the room we happen to be in today" (p. 84). This is salient for research endeavors, which are mired in asymmetrical information-gathering relationships, and speaks to the broader purposes of research itself: to not merely contribute to documenting existing inequities but to question and transform educational arrangements.

CBRE privileges coming together in a common cause of educational equity as a striving ideal, but it does not romanticize the process. It entails practices of coalitional work that do not subscribe to either a facile consensus that transcends power dynamics, or a realpolitik of interest convergence guided by instrumental calculations. We believe there are two important considerations in conceptualizing and undertaking coalitional research. The first is what Táíwò (2020) describes as the "elite capture" of identity politics and social justice pursuits. Táíwò writes,

> A key problem with elite capture is that the subgroup of people with power over and access to the resources that get used to describe, define, and create political realities—in other words, elites—are substantively different from the total set of people affected by the decisions they make. As the part of the group closest to power and resources, they are typically the part

whose interests overlap with the total group's the least. In the absence of the right kind of checks or constraints, they will capture the group's values, forcing people to coordinate on a narrower social project than the group would if power were distributed differently. When elites run the show, the "group's" interests get whittled down to what they have in common with those at the top.

(2020, para. 22)

When bringing people together to engage in joint research, there is a danger that the complexities of political priorities and of people's experiences can get flattened and narrowed, co-opted by those with most power within the group. This has implications for intra-group dynamics (whose perspectives are listened to, how common projects are formed and carried out, etc.) as well as who is considered a partner in the first place. Research-practice partnerships, for example, could continue to privilege particular stakeholders, such as those with most power in both academia and sites of educational practice such as school districts, without extending the right to research to those outside such particular "rooms," like the vast majority of teachers, youth, and families. Another danger of elite capture in CBRE is that the interests of the community become absorbed by the neoliberal agendas of those with the most power.

Both internal and external dynamics are important considerations for coalitional research, which require reflexivity about how power shapes common projects. How do people across boundaries, impacted by interlocking yet differing oppressions, come together in the service of a constructive politics? We believe that communities of inquiry across differences call for what feminist philosopher María Lugones (2006) describes as "complex communication" rooted in interdependence, care, polyvocality, and opacity. Lugones challenges the notion that coalition happens through speaking transparently or in one voice—we can imagine that a singular narrative, perspective, or research priority is subject to power asymmetries and elite capture—but that does not mean that coalition is not possible. Lugones proposes deep coalitions among the oppressed as occurring through complex communication; these are "coalitions that are based on processes of estrangement and mutual transformation" (Medina, 2020, p. 214). Rather than "assimilating the text of others to our own," Lugones (2006) argues that complex communication "is enacted through a change in one's own vocabulary, one's sense of self, one's way of living, in the extension of one's collective memory, through developing forms of communication that signal disruption of the reduction attempted by the oppressor" (p. 84). These communities thus entail "traveling" to the interpretive horizons of others, unsettling our own understandings, and developing new ways of speaking as we "create and cement relational identities" (p. 84) in the process of collaboration. Pairing scholarship with social organizing means recognizing that our research together is a social practice which can never be neutral. We try to be self-reflective about the ways in which we are located in the messiness of the world; we also engage the world politically in a manner that, we suggest, does not compromise our work's status as research but rather creates the conditions for collectively embodying the kinds of educational justice we investigate and enact together.

Returning to our opening vignette, we can understand Lukas' and Ivy's involvement on the panel as an example of complex communication in the service of education and housing justice. They worked alongside other, differently situated, colleagues to interrogate the systemic causes of dispossession that impact both Black and Immigrant communities, the underlying oppressive logics which rationalize, for example, the closing of a neighborhood school and the eviction of tenants in an affordable housing project, without flattening their respective experiences. Throughout their research process, they were not interested in "knowing" others as much as learning alongside others, "traveling" to new interpretive horizons.

We thus understand "community" not as a given, but heterogenous, and permeable, with shifting boundaries and with possibilities for making and re-making. Researching from the location of communities underscores that there is no place of purity from which to engage in social analysis and advocacy. Every person has some relationship to larger, intersectional systems of oppression, including racism, heteronormative patriarchy, ableism, class exploitation, and nativism. We conduct research from the messiness and contradictions of the social world, and thus CBRE is forthright that it is a form of immanent critique and praxis.

Ultimately, community-based research is a collaboration between people. Our own partnership began directly with families who were affiliated with a faith-based organization. Over the years the leadership of the church and affiliated non-profit organization which helped to mediate the partnership has changed, but our relationships with the families have sustained and even expanded to include individuals from across the city. Research that seeks to address educational inequities will necessarily involve unstable conditions, where neighborhoods may change or disappear, leadership fluctuates, schools shutter, individuals are detained or deported, and partnering organizations struggle to keep the lights on. These adverse conditions present challenges in carrying out CBRE but are also CBRE's raison d'etre: to play a role, however modest, in the survival and thriving of people existing in systems that produce economic and social precarity.

A commitment to a CBRE project, therefore, may not follow a conventional academic timeline. It is not necessarily over when the data has been collected and analyzed, because it is about being accountable to others and the larger community. In fact, CBRE should end at any moment, even before any research has been completed, if those with whom one partners no longer find the collaboration useful or if there has been a significant breach of trust. Community members also have the right to "refuse" exploitive relationships (Simpson, 2014). CBRE is a verb and an ongoing option that partners continually cultivate.

Questions for Reflection

1. Which intellectual legacies and theories of knowledge inform your CBRE?
2. How does power circulate through the research collaboration in your context?
3. How does the research advance the interests and desires of those most directly impacted by educational injustices? How is the CBRE part of a constructive agenda for social change and transformation?

Note

1 Naming is a political issue. Throughout this book, we use pseudonyms for many individuals who have been involved in the project. A few adults feel strongly about claiming their names and identities as a condition for research, and we have respected their wishes.

References

Alcoff, L. M. (2006). *Visible identities: Race, gender, and the self*. Oxford University Press.

Anzaldúa, G. (1999). *Borderlands/la frontera: The new mestiza* (2nd ed.). Aunt Lute Books.

Appadurai, A. (2006). The right to research. *Globalization, Societies, and Education*, *4*(2), 167–177.

Arendt, H. (1976). *The origins of totalitarianism*. Harcourt.

Baker-Bell, A. (2020). "We been knowin": Toward an antiracist language & literacy education. *Journal of Language and Literacy Education*, *16*(1), 1–12.

Bakhtin, M. (1984). *Problems of Dostoevsky's poetics* (C. Emerson, Trans. & Ed.). University of Minnesota Press.

Baldwin, D. (2021). *In the shadow of the ivory tower: How universities are plundering our cities*. Bold Type Books.

Butler, J. (2004). *Precarious life: The powers of mourning and violence*. Verso.

Cahill, C. (2007). Including excluded perspectives in participatory action research. *Design Studies*, *28*(3), 325–340.

Caine, V., & Mill, J. (2016). *Essentials of community-based research*. Routledge.

Cammarota, J., & Fine, M. (2008). Youth participatory action research: A pedagogy for transformational resistance. In J. Cammarota & M. Fine (Eds.), *Revolutionizing education: Youth participatory action research in motion* (pp. 1–11). Routledge.

Campano, G. (2007). *Immigrant students and literacy: Reading, writing, and remembering*. Teachers College Press.

Campano, G., Ghiso, M. P., Badaki, O., & Kannan, C. (2020). Agency as collectivity: Community-based research for educational equity. *Theory Into Practice*, *59*(2). https://doi.org/10.1080/00405841.2019.1705107

Campano, G., Medina, C. L., Thomas, E. E., & Stornaiuolo, A. (2021). Literacy and imperialism. *Research in the Teaching of English*, *56*(2), 125–131.

Campano, G., & Simon, R. (2010). Practitioner research as resistance to the normal curve. In C. Dudley-Marling & A. Gurn (Eds.), *The myth of the normal curve (Disability studies in education)* (pp. 221–239). Peter Lang.

Caraballo, L., Lozenski, B., Lyiscott, J. J., & Morrell, E. (2017). YPAR and critical epistemologies: Rethinking education research. *Review of Research in Education, 41*, 311–336.

Caraballo, L., & Lyiscott, J. (2020). Collaborative inquiry: Youth, social action, and critical qualitative research. *Action Research, 18*(2), 194–211.

Clapham, A. (2015). *Human rights: A very short introduction.* Oxford University Press.

Cochran-Smith, M., & Lytle, S. L. (1999). The teacher research movement: A decade later. *Educational researcher, 28*(7), 15–25.

Cochran-Smith, M., & Lytle, S. L. (2009). *Inquiry as stance: Practitioner research for the next generation.* Teachers College Press.

Combahee River Collective (2014). A Black feminist statement. *Women's Studies Quarterly, 42*(3–4), 271–280.

Crenshaw, K. W. (2017). *On intersectionality: Essential writings.* The New Press.

de los Ríos, C. V., Martinez, D. C., Musser, A. D., Canady, A., Camangian, P., & Quijada, P. D. (2019). Upending colonial practices: Toward repairing harm in English education. *Theory Into Practice, 58*(4), 359–367.

de los Ríos, C. V., & Molina, A. (2020). Literacies of refuge: "Pidiendo posada" as ritual of justice. *Journal of Literacy Research, 52*(1), 32–54.

Fine, M. (2008). An epilogue, of sorts. In J. Cammarota & M. Fine (Eds.), *Revolutionizing education: Youth participatory action research in motion* (pp. 213–234). Routledge.

Fine, M. (2018). *Just research in contentious times: Widening the methodological imagination.* Teachers College Press.

Fregoso, R. L. (2014). For a pluriversal declaration of human rights. *American Quarterly, 66*(3), 583–608.

Freire, P. (1970). *Pedagogy of the oppressed.* Continuum.

Gadsden, V. L., & Dixon-Román, E. J. (2017). "Urban" schooling and "urban" families: The role of context and place. *Urban Education, 52*(4), 431–459.

Ghiso, M. P. (2016). The Laundromat as the transnational local: Young children's literacies of interdependence. *Teachers College Record, 118*(1), 1–46.

Glissant, E. (1997). *Poetics of relation* (B. Wing, Trans.). University of Michigan Press.

Gultom, F., Gulton, F., Kosasih, M., Li, M., Lie, J., Lorenzo, C., Hidayat, F., Peralta Rios, O., Perez, E., Ponce, M., Setiawan, D., Setiawan, O., Zhinin, B., Sengbounpheng, P., Colson, Y., Ward, S., Thakurta, A., Kannan, C., Narron, L., Vazquez Ponce, O., & Campano, G. (2019). What is home? A collaborative multimodal inquiry project by transnational youth in South Philadelphia. *In:Cite Journal, 1*(2), 4–24.

Hames-García, M. (2011). *Identity complex: Making the case for multiplicity.* University of Minnesota Press.

Harney, S., & Moten, F. (2013). *The undercommons: Fugitive planning and Black study.* Minor Compositions.

Larson, J., & Moses, R. (Eds.). (2015). *Community literacies and shared resources for transformation.* Routledge.

Lorde, A. (1984). *Sister outsider: Essays and speeches.* Crossing Press.

Love, B. (2023). *Punished for dreaming: How school reform harms Black children and how we heal.* St. Martin's Press.

Lugones, M. (2006). On complex communication. *Hypatia, 21*(3), 75–85.

Lytle, S. L. (2008). At last: Practitioner inquiry and the practice of teaching: Some thoughts on "better". *Research in the Teaching of English, 42*(3), 373–379.

Madhok, S. (2021). *Vernacular rights cultures: The politics of origins, human rights, and gendered struggles for justice.* Cambridge University Press.

Marciano, J. E., Peralta, L. M., Lee, J. S., Rosemurgy, H., Holloway, L., & Bass, J. (2020). Centering community: Enacting culturally responsive-sustaining YPAR during COVID-19. *Journal of Multicultural Education*, *14*(2), 163–175.

Medina, J. (2020). Complex communication and decolonial struggles: The forging of deep coalitions through emotional echoing and resistant imaginations. *Critical Philosophy of Race*, *8*(1–2), 212–236.

Mignolo, W. (2000). *Local histories/global designs: Coloniality, subaltern knowledges, and border thinking*. Princeton University Press.

Mignolo, W. (2011). I am where I think: Remapping the order of knowing. In F. Lionnet & S. Shih (Eds.), *The creolization of theory* (pp. 159–192). Duke University Press.

Mirra, N., Garcia, A., & Morrell, E. (2015). *Doing youth participatory action research: Transforming inquiry with educators, researchers, and students*. Routledge.

Mohanty, S. P. (1997). *Literary theory and the claims of history: Postmodernism, objectivity, multicultural politics*. Cornell University Press.

Mohanty, S. P. (2018). Social justice and culture: On identity, intersectionality, and epistemic privilege. In G. Craig (Ed.), *The handbook of global social justice* (pp. 418–427). Elgard.

Moraga, C., & Anzaldúa, G. (Eds.). (1983). *This bridge called my back: Writings of radical women of color*. Kitchen Table/Women of Color Press.

Morrell, E. (2008). Six summers of YPAR: Learning, action, and change in urban education. In J. Cammarota & M. Fine (Eds.), *Revolutionizing education: Youth participatory action research in motion* (pp. 155–184). Routledge.

Moya, P. (2002). *Learning from experience: Minority identities, multicultural struggles*. University of California Press.

Moya, P. (2011). Who we are and from where we speak. *Transmodernity: Journal of Peripheral Cultural Production in the Luso-Hispanic World*, *1*(2), 79–94.

Moyn, S. (2012). *The last utopia: Human rights in history*. Harvard University Press.

Nasir, N. I. (2012). *Racialized identities: Race and achievement among African American youth*. Stanford University Press.

Oliveira, G. (2018). *Motherhood across borders: Immigrants and their children in Mexico and New York*. New York University Press.

Parikh, C., & Matlin, N. (2015). Human rights and the tautology of human being. In A. S. Moore & E. S. Goldberg (Eds.), *Teaching human rights in literary and cultural studies* (pp. 27–38). Modern Language Association.

Patel, L. (2013). *Youth held at the border: Immigration, education and the politics of inclusion*. Teacher College Press.

Paul, M. (2023). *The ends of freedom: Reclaiming America's lost promise of economic rights*. University of Chicago Press.

Penuel, W. R., & Gallagher, D. J. (2017). *Creating research-practice partnerships in education*. Harvard Education Press.

Rodríguez, D. (2020). *White Reconstruction: Domestic warfare and the logics of genocide*. Fordham University Press.

Rodríguez, N., Enriquez, G., Sambolín Morales, A., & Torres, A. (2021). In dialogue: Literacy and imperialism: The Filipinx and Puerto Rican experience. *Research in the Teaching of English*, *56*(2), 223–230.

Rusoja, A. (2017). *We are our own best advocates: Latinx immigrants teaching and learning for their rights* (Publication No. 10273554) [Doctoral Dissertation, University of Pennsylvania]. ProQuest Dissertations Publishing.

Sealey-Ruiz, Y. (2021). The critical literacy of race: Toward racial literacy in urban teacher education. In H. R. Milner & K. Lomotey (Eds.), *Handbook of urban education* (pp. 281–295). Routledge.

Siebers, T. (2007). Disability and the right to have rights. *Disability Studies Quarterly, 27*(1–2), 19–19.

Simpson, A. (2014). *Mohawk interruptus: Political life across the borders of settler states*. Duke University Press.

Smith, L. T. (2021). *Decolonizing methodologies: Research and indigenous people* (3rd ed.). Bloomsbury.

Stoecker, R. (2009). Are we talking the walk of community-based research? *Action Research, 7*(4), 385–404.

Strand, K., Marullo, S., Cutforth, N., Stoecker, R., & Donohue, P. (2003). Outstanding. *Michigan Journal of Community Service Learning, 9*(1), 5–15.

Strong, K., Walker, S., Wallace, D., Sriprakash, A., Tikly, L., & Soudien, C. (2023). Learning from the movement for Black lives: Horizons of racial justice for comparative and international education. *Comparative Education Review, 67*(S1), S1–S24.

Táíwò, O. O. (2020, May 7). Identity politics and elite capture. *Boston Review.* https://bostonreview.net/articles/olufemi-o-taiwo-identity-politics-and-elite-capture/

Táíwò, O. O. (2022). *Elite capture: How the powerful took over identity politics (and everything else)*. Haymarket Books.

Vasudevan, L., & Campano, G. (2009). The social production of risk and the promise of adolescent literacies. *Review of Research in Education, 33*(1), 310–353.

Yosso, T. J. (2005). Whose culture has capital? A critical race theory discussion of community cultural wealth. *Race, Ethnicity, and Education, 8*(1), 69–91.

3 What Does It Mean to Partner?

New Images of the Engaged Scholar

This chapter invites reflection about the motivations to engage in CBRE and explores how power dynamics are entangled throughout research collaborations. Partnership research does not solve all educational problems. Rather, they have the potential to be "constructive disruptions" (Cochran-Smith & Lytle, 2009, p. 33) of university and school cultures. Community-based partnerships are cultivated and enacted through social practices that are responsive to community interests. Thus, key methodological tenets like developing trust, gaining access, determining research directions, and implementing research designs and goals are continuously negotiated as partnerships develop, deepen, and change. While that means that there are no templates to follow can guarantee a "good" partnership, we do believe certain virtues are necessary for CBRE—which set the foundation for the responsive and iterative practices that form part of any equitable research relationship.

CBRE is premised on a sense of belonging. From our experiences, everyone who is involved in CBRE needs to know they are making unique contributions to the work. In the CARE Initiative we believe that all our stories matter; all our perspectives and talents matter; we are all singularly invaluable, if however flawed, pieces of a whole, to paraphrase Elaine Castillo (2022). Community members have reiterated this sentiment in many variations over the years. One of the Latine elders in the CARE Initiative put it beautifully, noting: "We are interconnected, and linked, like a chain" (Campano et al., 2013). The "community" in community-based research is thus taken very seriously. It is not the same as a research team where individuals' various competencies are leveraged to instrumentally complete the research cycle, and mentorship is enacted as a hierarchical form of apprenticeship into the profession (Ghiso et al., 2019). In CBRE, we are all mentoring one another because everyone's commitment to the work *is* the work, and one's intellectual community expands beyond academia.

DOI: 10.4324/9781003279686-3

CBRE and Self-Reflexivity

How might researchers prepare themselves for this kind of relationally demanding and egalitarian form of collective inquiry, especially in institutional contexts that reward competition and individual distinction? University-based researchers, including graduate students, ought to be provided opportunities to reflect on their intellectual and emotional investments in CBRE. They may ask themselves questions such as the following: What drives my desire to do this kind of work? What connections, if any, do I have to the communities with whom I do research and the issues they/we are exploring? How did I find myself in collaboration with this community at this time? How does CBRE speak to my larger commitments, not just as a scholar but as a citizen of the world?

The intellectual historian Dominick LaCapra, who has applied psychoanalytic concepts to methodology in the discipline of history, identifies several tendencies that researchers may enact in their relationships with the topic or people they are researching (Goldberg, 1998)—or, in the case of CBRE, researching alongside. On one pole, they may assume a type of exaggerated clinical distance that denies their own affective investments in their "object" of study, perhaps to perpetuate an aura of scholarly authority. On the other pole, researchers, through transferential relationships, may over-identify with those with whom they work, for example, re-enacting traumas they are exploring or even misrepresenting their own experiences in order to procure an "authenticity" or proximity to community concerns. To some degree, these tendencies may be inevitable as everyone's identities are shaped by both the institutions within which they work and their relationships with others, and we speculate that there may be a range of other psychodynamics at play that are beyond our ken. No one engages in research from a position of ideological neutrality. But it is important for researchers to explicitly reflect on these dynamics and be self-aware of what histories, both personal and group, and affective intensities they invariably bring to the research process.

Gerald, for example, had a (minor) epiphany—later in his career—which may provide an example of the subtleties of his own emotional stakes in CBRE. He had familiarized himself with recent psychological research on mixed-race people, who are disproportionality diagnosed with mental health issues because they may not conform to societal binaries of identity and are often lonely because they do not feel they have a community or a people. This scholarship resonated with Gerald's own experiences and with many of his family and friends who self-identify as biracial as well. He realized that what motivates his own commitment to participatory research approaches over the years may be, in part, a desire to create the community which has never felt fully present in his life, to fill an absence. This desire could potentially place an unfair burden on his collaborators if gone unchecked. Our research partners are not, of course, here to fix us. This does not imply that the nuances of Gerald's biracial experiences are a detriment to research; they may be utilized as a strength: for example, informing his sensitivity to scapegoating in group dynamics, nourishing his commitment to inclusivity, and shaping a pluralistic intellectual and cultural disposition perhaps appropriate for a transnational, multiethnic research team. In research, as in life, it is how we interpret and utilize our experiences that matters. Given the interpersonal boundary-crossing nature of CBRE, it is especially untenable for university-based researchers to hide behind a disinterested veneer of scholarly authority. But as we bring our fuller selves into our research, it is equally important to do so with professional integrity and self-awareness.

Virtues of Critical Empathy, Epistemic Pluralism, and Solidarity

All researchers ought to approach CBRE with respect for the agency of those with whom they collaborate. No one researcher, or community leader for that matter, "speaks for" or empowers others in the research process; people empower themselves, and researchers ought to be cautious about perpetuating a type of secular missionary ideology. While there are reciprocal university collaborations, there are also many partnerships based on transmission models, where researchers, for example, roll out best practices to be implemented without understanding community nuances or the knowledge, interests, and goals of those who are meant to benefit from their interventions. And, unfortunately, there are histories of exploitive, extractive, and harmful research inflicted upon communities. Even the most well-meaning and careful university-based researchers carry these institutional histories with them, and it is no surprise, and certainly justified, when community members are skeptical of potential university partners. Several CARE Initiative members have indeed expressed that they have felt exploited by researchers who have extracted data and left without returning to report on the benefits of the research to the community. They have discussed how research instruments felt imposed on them and were culturally insensitive. These types of experiences have rightly attuned communities to the power hierarchies and unidirectionality of much university-led research. CBRE needs to listen to and learn from these harmful histories in order to construct a stronger foundation for partnership research.

Ideally, scholars seeking to engage in CBRE gain ever-deepening understandings of the social and political complexities of research partnerships and develop a conceptual vocabulary to make an argument about addressing these through participatory methodologies. An openness to learning from others requires relational epistemic humility (Alcoff, 2022): ongoing self-reflexivity about the limits of one's own knowledge and assumptions while embracing the importance of multiple perspectives, especially from community members themselves.

Because CBRE involves significant relational labor, over the years we have found that successful researchers embody three important virtues: *critical empathy*, *epistemic pluralism*, and *solidarity*.

- *Critical Empathy* begins with reflecting on distinctions between self and other to better understand and learn from others' experiences. Empathy must work through—rather than evade or homogenize—difference. The word "critical" suggests an empathy that is attentive to power dynamics and injustices that differentially impact and cause harm to people based on intersectional aspects of their identities and experiences (e.g., Lobb, 2017).
- *Epistemic pluralism* acknowledges that there are multiple ways of knowing and conveying one's knowledge, thus challenging established intellectual hierarchies. Educators, activists, and researchers engage in pedagogies which leverage such pluralism, such as ones involving drama (e.g., Medina & Campano, 2006), comics (e.g., Low, 2017), photography (e.g., Ghiso et al., 2019) and multimodal forms of inquiry.
- *Solidarity* requires that university-based researchers "espouse the aspirations of the organization with which they are collaborating, both by placing people's knowledge on an equal footing with academic knowledge and by embracing the political objectives of the groups with which they are working" (Rappaport, 2020, p. xix). CBRE researchers not only embrace larger political objectives, such as immigrant rights, but, following feminist theorists including Maria Lugones (2003), also express their solidarity in the quotidian, such as supporting youth in their college essay, parents in advocating for better language services, or families in interpreting and resisting bureaucracies which criminalize them, like truancy letters (Campano et al., 2013).

While many people drawn to collaborative research may already exhibit these virtues, we believe they are not essential traits of individuals, but rather dispositions and skills that can be developed through CBRE.

The Stories That Bring Us to CBRE

Not unlike activist organizing, CBRE will involve the cooperation of people who occupy various social locations and hold different degrees and forms of privilege. This entails ongoing self-reflection about one's own identity vis-à-vis others in the collaboration, beyond an obligatory "statement of positionality" where one comes clean about one's identity and leaves it at that. One space where graduate students may reflect on their motives to engage in CBRE is the dissertation or research proposal, and specifically a section of the proposal called "the story of the question." Although we do not know the origins of this section, we were introduced to it, along with generations of other students, from our mentor Dr. Susan L. Lytle. The idea of a "story of the question" is to explore and reflect on how one has arrived at the research they hope to conduct alongside others, be they educators, families, or youth. One of its assumptions is that research questions do not need to come from a "gap in the literature," but rather emerge from processes of Freirean problem-posing in sites of practice and organizing. The story of the question is typically written with the "I" (or "we", in our case), providing an initial venue to reflect on one's own identity, motive, and affective investments in one's envisioned research. This "I," however, is invariably a dialogical "I," shaped by others and always in the act of becoming.

Part of the story of the CARE Initiative, for example, is that when we (María Paula & Gerald) returned to Philadelphia, we wanted to learn about immigration activism in the city because of our own transnational backgrounds and prior experiences as teachers in diverse city schools with large populations of students from immigrant, migrant, and refugee backgrounds. We attended numerous actions and events throughout the city, including a Know Your Rights workshop at a South Philadelphia Catholic parish. After the workshop, leaders from the Indonesian community, upon learning of our own backgrounds and work, asked if we might consider a partnership. "Education" they told us, is "what gives our community hope." Over a decade later the partnership persists. Importantly, the first year or so of the partnership involved no research. We initially spent time trying to support families in their current initiatives, such as a community health fair organized by the Concerned Black Catholics, a family literacy night attended by hundreds of people, a pen pal exchange between Gerald's Masters students and children from the Indonesian Sunday school, and potluck in the park co-organized by the Vietnamese and Indonesian youth groups. This period set a foundation of trust, and gave us time to see how, if at all, our work as educational researchers might be useful to the community. It also allowed us, over time, to reflect on how our own immigrant backgrounds and teaching experiences intersected with and differed from those of children and families in South Philadelphia, and to see if we could write a collectively composed new story with the community we were getting to know.

Over the years we have mentored many students in CBRE. In the sections that follow, we share excerpts from several of their "stories of the question" as examples of the genre as well as how the respective authors—Grace Player, Alicia Rusoja, and Gordon Dee Asaah—illustrate the scholarly virtues we believe to be necessary for CBRE. They, like other students we have had the fortune to teach and learn alongside, wrote remarkable dissertations and continue to be involved in meaningful and impactful research partnerships with communities. A few things to note before sharing their words. They all had experiences as educators, organizers, and artists prior to entering graduate studies. They intentionally applied to doctoral programs where they would have the opportunity to engage in participatory inquiry. Once in the doctoral program, they worked on the CARE Initiative for several years, gaining hands-on experience in CBRE methodologies, and even crafting, within the auspices of the larger research collaborative, pilot projects which combined their own emerging interests as scholars with the cares and concerns of families and youth. Finally, they proposed dissertation studies that overlapped with, or existed in proximity to, the CARE Initiative. Grace created an extracurricular girls of color writing community at the parish school. Alicia centered her research at a grassroots immigrant rights organization and worked alongside several families who had been involved in the CARE Initiative. Dee cultivated trust with ALOFO (Allies of Africa Organization), a non-profit community center supporting youth of African and Black Caribbean descent in education, health, and legal services that shared affinities with the community center at the parish. Dee began volunteering with ALOFO early in his graduate studies while simultaneously working on the CARE Initiative.

This background is important because it addresses a question regarding CBRE and research-practice partnerships more generally, especially for graduate students or scholars at the beginning stages of their careers. Partnerships take a long time to cultivate, and given the pressures to be productive and meet institutional metrics for success, shouldn't scholars wait until they are already established in the academy to devote themselves to this type of research? We have observed that many incoming students who are attracted to participatory inquiry will not wait to forge horizontal relationships with research collaborators until some nebulous time in the future; that would go against some of their most deeply held values and commitments. We thus believe it is important for advanced scholars to establish long-term collaborations with communities built on a foundation of trust and goodwill, where community participants have a strong sense of collective agency and authority over the terms of the partnership. These collaborations are a rich context within which graduate students, and scholars new to CBRE, can learn how to develop, sustain, and nurture research partnerships. By the time Grace, Alicia, and Dee proposed their dissertation research, for example, they had spent years immersed in the CARE Initiative and had gained experience in just about every aspect of the research process, from developing relationships with collaborators, facilitating communities of inquiry, collecting/analyzing data, and going public with findings through presentations and publications. They also encountered and worked through real-world issues of power alongside a team of university and community-based researchers committed to mentoring and learning from and alongside them. The CARE Initiative thus serves as a cornerstone for doctoral students' own inquiries and collaborative research.

Grace Player: Girls of Color Centering Solidarity, Joy, and Celebration

Grace's story of the question exemplifies a scholar whose research interests are unapologetically driven by her political convictions and commitments. She writes that her proposed research is "the manifestation of many of the passions, struggles, and questions that have arisen from my life experiences … as a mixed race, Asian woman … An examination of both the privileges and the burdens that result from this identification play into my work." Grace discusses the transnational familial history of her Japanese-Brazilian mother to explore how "a world dominated by whiteness and masculinity" impacts girls of color but also how "girls of color are brave, brilliant, and beautiful in the face of these inequities." Grace's display of empathy, however, comes not from eliding difference. She explicitly draws inspiration from Yuri Kochiyama and Grace Lee Boggs to examine how the privileges and burdens of her own identity, as well as many non-Black POC, are complicit with anti-Black racism. This form of empathy, one that embraces difference, is a precondition for genuine solidarity (Lorde, 1984), what Grace, in her study, refers to as "sisterhood" (Player, 2021).

Grace's dissertation was designed to be responsive to the girls' desire to have a space outside of official schooling to investigate their experiences because in school it was not safe to do so. She thus followed the youth's leads. Grace dissertation research would explicitly investigate both the possibilities and challenges of Black and Asian girls cultivating solidarity across difference (Player, 2018). In her story of the question, however, Grace did leave out one important aspect of her identity. She is, herself, an incredible artist. Her expansive notion of what constitutes a feminist writing pedagogy includes the arts as well as multimodal forms of representation, something she would continue to develop throughout her career. In fact, while writing this chapter, we received word that Grace, in her capacity as a professor, has developed a youth driven arts collective, where girls of color are "visionaries and curators of liberatory art spaces" (Player, 2023). It is a rich example of the virtue of epistemic pluralism—using the arts as a form of meaning-making—as well as evidence that, increasingly, newer scholars are feeling more empowered to engage in creative and participatory forms of inquiry, a trend we hope continues in the field.

Alicia Rusoja: Collective Teaching, Learning, and Organizing for Immigrant Rights

In her story of the question, Alicia discusses her "visceral" connection to the immigrant rights movement as "a Latina immigrant in the U.S., and as a community and intergenerational educator/organizer." She also shares a poignant vignette of leaving Venezuela as a child: "It was difficult for me to learn English, it was difficult to get used to living here, and I felt so much sadness and anger." Like Grace, she also conveys empathy, drawing distinctions between experiences. If her own immigration was challenging, Alicia affords her participant co-researchers a certain right to opacity (Glissant, 1997), explaining that "she can't begin to conceive how difficult it is for fellow immigrants … who are forced to live through violations to their human rights in the US that comes with not having immigration papers." Alicia then poses several questions exploring how she might research and organize alongside families who have different immigrant, racialized, and class-based experiences than herself, including: "How do I, and we, engage this struggle in a reflexive way, where our teaching, learning, and organizing practices constantly improve and contribute to achieving a long-term shared vision of equity and justice?" For Alicia, as for many of the students we have mentored, relationships of respectful solidarity with communities are nonnegotiable, and more important than the research itself, should they ever come into conflict.

A working presupposition of Alicia's is that intergenerational organizing is a form of research: knowing about the world's inequities is inseparable from envisioning how to change them for the better. She thus challenges and disrupts academia's claims to having a monopoly on knowledge and expertise. Alicia's commitment to "communal pedagogy" (Rusoja, 2017) and inquiry has proven to be much more than academic verbalism. Alicia has maintained close, reciprocal relationships with the co-researchers of her dissertation over the years, several of whom have become school educators and entered academia themselves. They have continued to research, write, and organize together through the arts, storytelling, protests, bus rides, cooking, sharing meals, as well as more conventional academic publications (Rusoja et al., 2023), forms of epistemic pluralism that make research a more communal endeavor.

Dee Asaah: Multimodal Inquiry with African and Caribbean Youth

Dee's collaboration with youth from ALOFO, a local African diaspora community organization, brought together several strands of his life's work. As he explains in his story of the question, Dee runs a community-based non-profit in his home country of Cameroon to support the education of students displaced by a civil war which has upended his country. He characterizes his dissertation research as "personal," and writes that it "emanates from my own experiences as a lifelong member of minoritized communities; a student under two colonial systems of education in Cameroon; a multilingual, transnational student in Europe and the United States; and the parent of two Black teenage high schoolers in the U.S. K-12 education system." Dee, like many of the doctoral students we have worked with, would be involved in advocating for students in his larger community—the Black African diaspora—irrespective of the professional, institutional, or geographical context of his work. He understands many aspects of the students' lives because he, too, has had to navigate a schooling that primitivized his "ancestral ways of knowing and being," such as "dance, music, and traditional rituals." Yet, he also recognizes that his experiences as "a graduate student at elite American universities" are different from the ALOFO youth, and index power dynamics he had to wrestle with as he carried out his dissertation research.

Dee opens his story of the question with a vignette of how one of the ALOFO youth has been marginalized in schools for not speaking "adequate English." The student does in fact speak English, as well as several other languages, including French and Madingo. Dee, a polyglot himself, was thus concerned that the ALOFO students were not able to bring their "whole selves" into school, and leverage their vast linguistic, cultural, semiotic, and epistemic repertoires. As an artist who has professional expertise in film production, Dee was able to embrace epistemic pluralism as a corrective to the ways that school pedagogies narrowed and buried youth's talents and experiences. Dee proposed a CBRE project where the youth could employ creative multimodal forms of inquiry to interrogate their own schooling, claim their own agency, and define future success for themselves. In the spirit of empathy and solidarity, Dee also supported the non-profit in pivoting to online programming during the Covid-19 pandemic, drawing on his knowledge as well as institutional resources for technology platforms which were out-of-reach for many community organizations.

Through the stories of their questions, graduate students may be engaging in what Yolanda Sealey-Ruiz would refer to as an "archeology of the self" (Sealey-Ruiz, 2021), "the process of digging deeply and 'peeling back the layers' on one's life experiences … to think in great depth about the way race and other issues of diversity live within them" (p. 288). Sealey-Ruiz names the archaeology of the self as central to developing racial literacies. Excavating the stories that draw us to and shape our work in CBRE means wrestling with the complexities of our intersectional identities, including the ways we are complicit with systems of oppression but also heirs to legacies of resistance. For the graduate students who have been involved in the CARE Initiative, this has meant not suppressing aspects of one's identity—as an artist, activist, educator, or cultural and racialized being—in order to conduct research intended to make an impact beyond the walls of the university, an orientation which challenges dominant approaches to academic socialization. We have found that partnership research brings to the fore the tensions and possibilities of becoming a community-engaged scholar, as graduate students contend with the interplay between their knowledge and interests, the expectations of the academy, and the concerns and goals of research partnerships.

Negotiating Power Dynamics

The virtues we've described are necessary for developing the skills to address issues of power and transform existing hierarchies in research. In this section, we share several examples of the types of power dynamics we ourselves have had to negotiate in CBRE. The critical incidents we have had to work through are not always predictable. Being situated in academia, with its emphasis on DEI training, would lead us to think that many of the issues of power would entail the need for individuals associated with the university to reflect on their individual privilege (class-based, racialized, educational) vis-à-vis researchers from the community. While this type of reflection is, of course, important, it is not a new consideration for members of the CARE Initiative, many of whom share some affinities, in their own backgrounds, with the communities they work alongside. Our most difficult challenges have had to do with academia's valuing of individual distinction, which may incentivize researchers to co-opt the knowledge and labor of others.

One initial crisis during the early stages of our partnership occurred when the research center of a senior colleague, with significant institutional power, caught wind of the CARE partnership from a presentation we made on campus. Because our work was situated at a Catholic church, members of the university center scheduled a meeting with some of the parish leaders to explore their own potential collaboration, as they were interested in the role of religion in urban affairs. We were not consulted about the meeting and felt steamrolled because we had spent significant time cultivating relationships with families at the parish, which were now being leveraged by others. Why not talk with us first about what we had already learned? This case of a powerful researcher appropriating existing and hard-won relationships to gain access to community contexts stands in contrast with the ways that individuals with less institutional capital had previously been stymied in their efforts to collaborate. Soon we became aware that the colleague in question had conducted infamous, racist "research" that would provide a scholarly justification for the prison industrial complex, and which encapsulated many of the extractivist and harmful research practices we were trying to fight against. At this point, we felt the need to intervene, and let families in the partnership know of this history so that they could make their own informed decision (ultimately, there was no collaboration).

The parish leaders could, of course, develop partnerships with whomever they wanted. And we could see how, from an institutional standpoint, this connection would seem to have made sense, without being privy to the specific ways such research had been used to harm communities of color. One important question for reflection is thinking about how decisions about partnering get made on the "university" side and the "community" side, both of which have their respective issues of power. Who is fielding decisions about research access? When different perspectives or tensions arise about partnering directions, how are they adjudicated? We were fortunate to have established a set of norms for CBRE (Campano, Ghiso, & Welch, 2015), and tenets such as "research should benefit the community" and "community member's knowledge and perspectives must be taken seriously" formed the foundation for deliberating whether partnership decisions aligned with these collective ideals. We share more about these norms in Chapter 4.

There have also been smaller incidences that nonetheless reflect deeper power dynamics. For example, a photographer from one of our universities once visited the parish to take pictures of our collaboration, which we appreciated because we didn't have the funds for such professional work. We later found out, however, that the photos were the property of the university, and several pictures of the doctoral students and youth were used in university magazines and professional talks, to brand the diversity of other colleagues' research projects. No one had explained to us, the doctoral students, or the youth that their images would be shared in this manner. While the families had signed permission slips for these images, our naïve working assumption was that they would only be used to represent the singular relationships we had all developed with one another in the context of our shared project. Instead, the photos became a stock resource that the university could use at their own discretion. It was another reminder that, as university faculty and students, we carry with us the university's priorities everywhere we go, irrespective of how thoughtful any one person is as an individual. As individuals involved in CBRE, however, our imperative is to enact ethical relationships, and when university policies and practices threaten to exploit or harm our partners, we must intervene.

Perhaps one of our most frustrating day-to-day challenges of CBRE has been compensating community members for their intellectual labor. We often invite our families to present their original research in our classes, which is invariably a powerful experience for the university students. While there is generally very little difficulty in providing honorariums to researchers from other universities who come to give a talk, it has been a different story for the youth or family researchers. We have found many bureaucratic hurdles to paying community researchers, even if the funds are readily available. Sometimes it has taken months, extensive paperwork, and innumerable back-and-forths to provide a relatively modest compensation to a youth researcher. This has even been the case for grant-funded projects premised on community partnerships, where compensation for community facilitation and expertise is a built-in expectation that is supported and encouraged. We are grateful and indebted to the thoughtful staff at our respective institutions who find ways to cut through this red tape. Community researchers are scholarly workers and deserve financial recognition. Unfortunately, many universities are just not designed to be in genuine partnership with them.

There are also, invariably, issues of power in the communities with whom university-based researchers collaborate. Communities are not homogenous and do not speak with a monolithic voice, despite often being invoked, by local leaders and university researchers alike, in essentializing terms. In earlier work (Campano, Ghiso, & Welch, 2016) we identified distinct, yet overlapping, sub-communities within the broader parish community where we originally began our partnership, including ones that focus on religious, social service, educational, activist, and cultural/linguistic initiatives within the parish. The various sub-communities reflected different centers of gravity and ethea with respect to the collective work of the parish, although any individual might be involved in several of them simultaneously. Critical incidents at the parish often had to do with a conflict and power struggle across, or sometimes within, these sub-communities. For example, the religious emphasis on a universalism and shared humanity, important for a broader multiracial congregation, sometimes led to a facile desire to transcend difference. This desire existed in tension with the urgency to address the distinct experiences of particular groups within the parish, such as the history of segregation, racism, and resistance of the Concerned Black Catholics. Likewise, there may be tensions between the programming goals of nonprofits, which value practical efficiency, and the research agenda of a university partnership, which requires time and disciplinary knowledge. In one instance, an issue arose when a volunteer who had been brought on to teach a language class for adults was utilizing materials from Ruby Payne, an approach we found to be racist and classist (Bomer et al., 2008). The service priority of the financially strained non-profit to provide low-cost or free programming conflicted with our own sense of what constitutes a high quality and anti-oppressive education. Yet the ways we typically preferred to co-construct curriculum with class participants was not feasible within the precarious structure of community organizations. As university-based researchers who are intentionally cultivating membership in the "community," we do not stand outside these dynamics. One of the biggest challenges of CBRE involves recognizing that dissonance and dissensus are epistemically productive and necessary for bringing about change, while simultaneously finding a way to forge a common vision and move forward.

Unsettling Binaries, Embracing Multiplicity

Following Audre Lorde (1984), one of the prerogatives for scholars engaged in CBRE is to be attentive to difference: different histories, identities, perspectives, ways of knowing and being, and social practices. It is only through difference that the community in community-based research can be genuinely forged and sustained. The working through of multiplicity and conflict is not only necessary to nurture relationships but, as discussed earlier, it is also an epistemic strength. We have continually encountered such moments, often in areas we did not predict beforehand. For example, during an inquiry into immigration, several of our Latine community leaders suggested that our research team attend an immigrant rights action at the State Capitol instead of one of our regularly scheduled gatherings at the parish, and many of us were excited about this proposal. It was a way of reinforcing our solidarity with members of our project who were undocumented and/or from mixed-status families. However, after we started organizing the trip, one of the Indonesian leaders from CARE called Dee, who was a doctoral student in the partnership at the time, to express their reservations. They said that several people in the Indonesian community were not comfortable attending the action. We had to remind ourselves that the respective communities were in different places regarding public protest, even if they were part of a shared struggle against oppressive border practices. The Latine families had a grassroots network of support for organizing and a local history of more visible forms of protest. The Indonesian families, by contrast, had not yet developed a similar form of politicized grassroots infrastructure. In addition, many of the elders in the community still harbored traumatic memories of sectarian violence and genocide in their home country, which was triggered by the prospects of political action. The community leaders reached out to Dee—we believe—because they knew he understood their feelings, having also immigrated from a wartorn country. Dee played a key role in resolving this potential conflict: We held two events, our regular scheduled gathering and an organized trip to the Capitol for those who were interested (which did in fact include members from across the cultural and linguistic communities in CARE). Looking back, this incident might have undermined our work together. But by bridging disparate perspectives, we were able to instead fortify bonds of trust. We were also able to gain a deeper and more nuanced understanding of one another's histories.

A similar situation occurred in navigating different perspectives on teaching within our research team. As new members enter the partnership, they bring varied experiences as educators—for example, in community organizing and adult popular education, as elementary or secondary teachers in a range of contexts (from charters to parochial schools to arts-based programs), and as teachers and curriculum developers in non-profit settings nationally and internationally. At the same time, the youth and intergenerational inquiry sessions in the CARE Initiative have also developed their own collective rhythm in response to community participation, an ebb and flow that balances school skills without being too school-like and that is unequivocally asset-based. Over the years, there have been instances where a facilitator's practices have been in tension with the group pedagogies or with community goals. We have taken these opportunities to reflect on what has influenced our ways of talking, teaching, and being with students. For example, how might having been educators in schools with zero-tolerance policies, or with heightened attention to performance measures impact our pedagogies in the moment, even if they are ostensibly geared toward equitable ends? Or how might our efforts toward constructivist or critical pedagogies be in tension with some community members' desires for more explicit emphasis on specific school-based skills?

These types of dilemmas have helped surface contrasting perspectives and not see them as inherently contradictory, but as openings to inform each other's thinking and the direction of our collective work. We have found that stepping back and taking time to individually and collectively inquire into differences as situated within particular histories and systems of relations has helped us navigate complex circumstances in dialogic ways. It has had increasing returns, with better understandings of one another and a culture of working through differences, making us all more apt to take multiple viewpoints seriously and to challenge one another with love and care.

Conclusion

CBRE is about people thinking and researching together across social and institutional boundaries to generate knowledge about collective educational flourishing. Doing this work within inherently unequal institutions and a flawed educational system means that we all are invariably complicit. But we can also do things better, if not perfectly. Reflecting on the methodological and ethical practices of the Civics Laboratory for Environmental Action Research

(CLEAR) lab, Max Liboiron (2021) writes that "doing anticolonial science within a dominant scientific context is simultaneously a commitment to dominant science and a divestment from it, which makes it uniquely compromised" (p. 134). In this framing, Liboiron's notion of compromise "is not a mistake or a failure" but rather "the condition for activism" (p. 134). Research that is community-led and attends to issues of justice invariably occurs within power asymmetries. As Liboiron aptly puts it, this means that "we are always caught up in the contradictions, injustices, and structures that already exist, that we have already identified as violent and in need of change" (p. 134). Our goals in CBRE are not to transcend these contradictions—an impossible task—but to know that choosing to do this work entails continuous collective deliberation amid inherent tensions.

Striving to make our way in compromised research in order to do things better, we have found, requires the aforementioned virtues of critical empathy, epistemic pluralism, and solidarity. There will be conflicts. While they often play themselves out as personal dramas, it is helpful to consider their systemic causes. What may seem like an individual or personal tension is often rooted in competing logics or responsibilities to which each of us may feel accountable. Within any given partnership, there will always be gatekeepers, contrasting personalities, oppressive practices, or toxic bureaucracies that could obstruct or derail the collaboration. It is important to work through these challenges while resisting the urge to scapegoat individuals (Girard, 1977), always keeping the collective goals for partnership at the forefront.

CBRE provides an image of the university scholar quite different from one who masters their discipline in order to critique from afar. Graduate students in the CARE Initiative have certainly gained disciplinary expertise—in our own case in the area of literacy studies. But they also cultivate a pedagogical and creative relationship to the discipline, imagining how this expertise can become realized in concrete contexts beyond the academic program, in places such as our partnership organization, and in relationship to the community members' own interests, epistemic practices, and resources. It is an image of the researcher as a cultural worker (Freire, 2005) who labors shoulder to shoulder with others, within the messiness of the world in all its contractions, to create new communities of inquiry and possibility.

Questions for Reflection

1. What are your investments in the partnership work you are doing (or seeking to do)? What is your own "story of the question"?
2. What are the virtues of the individuals with whom you work and how are these virtues valuable to the research?
3. What dilemmas and tensions are coming up in your work?

References

Alcoff, L. M. (2022). Extractivist epistemologies. *Tapuya: Latin American Science, Technology and Society*, *5*(1), 2127231.

Bomer, R., Dworin, J. E., May, L., & Semingson, P. (2008). Miseducating teachers about the poor: A critical analysis of Ruby Payne's claims about poverty. *Teachers College Record*, *110*(12), 2497–2531.

Campano, G., Ghiso, M. P., Yee, M., & Pantoja, A. (2013). Community research and coalitional literacy practices for educational justice. *Language Arts*, *90*(5), 314–326.

Campano, G., Ghiso, M. P., & Welch, B. (2015). Ethical and professional norms in community-based research. *Harvard Educational Review*, *85*(1), 29–49.

Campano, G., Ghiso, M. P., & Welch, B. (2016). *Partnering with immigrant communities: Action through literacy*. Teachers College Press.

Castillo, E. (2022). *How to read now: Essays*. Viking Press.

Cochran-Smith, M., & Lytle, S. L. (2009). *Inquiry as stance: Practitioner research for the next generation*. Teachers College Press.

Freire, P. (2005). *Teachers as cultural workers: Letters to those who dare teach*. Taylor and Francis.

Ghiso, M. P., Campano, G., Schwab, E., Asaah, G., & Rusoja, A. (2019). Mentoring in research-practice partnerships: Toward democratizing expertise. *AERA Open*, *5*(4), 1–12.

Ghiso, M. P., Martínez-Álvarez, P., Clayton, E., Álvarez, F., & Gutiérrez, M. (2019). Critical inquiry in the literacy curriculum: The community as transnational resources. *Language Arts*, *97*(2), 97–104.

Girard, R. (1977). *Violence and the sacred*. John Hopkins University Press.

Glissant, E. (1997). *Poetics of relation* (B. Wing, Trans.). University of Michigan Press.

Goldberg, A. (1998, June 9). *An interview with Professor Dominick LaCapra: "Acting out" and "working through" trauma*. Shoah Resource Center, The International School for Holocaust Studies. www.yadvashem.org/odot_pdf/Microsoft%20W ord%20-%203648.pdf

Liboiron, M. (2021). *Pollution is colonialism*. Duke University Press.

Lobb, A. (2017). Critical empathy. *Constellations: An International Journal of Critical and Democratic Theory*, *24*(4), 594–607.

Lorde, A. (1984). *Sister outsider: Essays and speeches*. Crossing Press.

Low, D. E. (2017). Students contesting" colormuteness" through critical inquiries into comics. *English Journal*, *106*(4), 19–28.

Lugones, M. (2003). *Pilgrimages/peregrinajes: Theorizing coalition against multiple oppressions*. Rowman & Littlefield.

Medina, C., & Campano, G. (2006). Performing identities through drama and teatro practices in multilingual classrooms. *Language Arts*, *84*(4), 332–341.

Player, G. D. (2018). *Unnormal sisterhood: Girls of color writing, reading, resisting, and being together*. (Publication No. 10843763). [Doctoral Dissertation, University of Pennsylvania]. ProQuest Dissertations Publishing.

Player, G. D. (2021). "My color of my name": Composing critical self-celebration with girls of color through a feminist of color writing pedagogy. *Research in the Teaching of English*, *55*(3), 216–240.

Player, G. D. (2023). *Curators of educational dreams: Girls of color as visionaries and creators of liberatory art spaces*. Spencer Foundation Racial Equity Research Grant.

Rappaport, J. (2020). *Cowards don't make history: Orlando Fals Borda and the origins of participatory action research*. Duke University Press.

Rusoja, A. (2017). *We are our own best advocates: Latinx immigrants teaching and learning for their rights* (Publication No. 10273554). [Doctoral Dissertation, University of Pennsylvania]. ProQuest Dissertations Publishing.

Rusoja, A., Portillo, Y., & Vazquez Ponce, O. (2023). "Mi lucha es tu lucha; tu lucha es mi lucha": Latinx immigrant youth organizers facilitating a new common sense through coalitional multimodal literacies. *International Journal of Qualitative Studies in Education, 36*(3), 487–507.

Sealey-Ruiz, Y. (2021). The critical literacy of race: Toward racial literacy in urban teacher education. In H. R. Milner & K. Lomotey (Eds.), *Handbook of urban education* (pp. 281–295). Routledge.

4   What Are the Ethics of CBRE?

Methodology as a Practice of Love

An Early Critical Incident

In one of the most significant experiences of my graduate studies several decades ago, I (Gerald) interviewed my lolo. The course assignment required interviewing someone familiar, and I selected my grandfather, a close, intimate relation who was also raised in a very different social milieu than myself. Having migrated in the 1920s as a colonial subject, young teenager, and orphan from the Mindanao region of the Philippines, then part of the "greater United States" (Immerwarh, 2019), my grandfather worked as a migrant laborer in California and eventually settled in New York City. This assignment was the first time in my formal schooling when I was encouraged to explore the Filipinx side of my identity, a schooling which had studiously elided or misrepresented the histories of a vast majority of humanity.

Learning from my grandfather was not something new, however. Throughout my childhood he had shared aspects of his life with me, especially regarding his experiences as a musician. I remember sitting next to him as he plucked his lap guitar, hearing about his gigs in various hotels throughout the city, and him displaying proudly the Campano name in the worn pages of the book of the American Federation of Musicians. We had improvised our own rhythm of intergenerational storying and learning over the years, but there was still so much I wanted to know, and as an adult I relished the opportunity to interview him. I remember meticulously crafting interview questions and making a special trip from my university to Queens, NYC, and ascending the stairwell of the walk-up apartment where my grandparents had raised seven children, my father the eldest. It was a pilgrimage I had made hundreds of times. Usually, I was buzzed in before I had a chance to press the doorbell, my grandparents spotting me in the courtyard from their window. I can still conjure the cooking aromas wafting through the stairwell and with it all the rituals of my visits, including the invariable offer of ginger ale from my grandmother and my grandfather insisting on relinquishing his reclining chair to the traveler.

Despite the comfort and familiarity of the environment, I felt nervous about the "fieldwork" exercise. In the process of trying to excavate a buried

DOI: 10.4324/9781003279686-4

familial history, I was bringing together two aspects of my life which until then had been compartmentalized: that of a graduate student and that of a grandchild, two ill-fitting pieces of a puzzle. My grandfather knew, of course, that I was interviewing him and was proud of my studies and my interest in documenting his life. He began our interview by graciously narrating his journey to California as a navy steward; his various migratory jobs planting trees and working on an oil tanker; the virulent racism he encountered on the west coast; his move to NYC; and his aspirations to become an actor but declining his first offered role as a Filipino houseboy in a production at a Brooklyn playhouse, and instead taking up job as an actual houseboy in Manhattan to provide for his family during the Depression. "I can do this job to survive," he conveyed to me, "but this does not define me. I won't be this stereotype on stage." Halfway through the interview, however, I began to realize that my scrawled fieldnotes might not suffice, and—aspiring to be diligent with my assignment—became concerned that I would not have an adequate transcript to analyze. When I reluctantly pulled out my tape recorder, then a symbol of my emerging identity as an official researcher, my nervousness morphed into apprehension. The recorder felt alienating, a type of extractive technology of othering. Although I didn't have the language at the time, I think I had an inchoate sense of the potential for epistemic object-ification in this minor research exercise: Was I taking his words out of our established lived relations and staging them—and by implication him—as an object to be theorized and classified? I am not sure if my grandfather felt the same way or if he just sensed my unease, but not too long after I pressed record, he proposed we take a break. "Don't worry Gerald," I remember him saying, "we will have plenty of time together to talk." I suspected this not to be true. He was in his nineties and faltering health. But I would later realize that he was right. I have been in dialogue with my grandfather my whole career, my whole life, even after he transitioned to the realm of the ancestors.

Over the years, my grandfather and I had developed our own organic ways of negotiating the co-construction of intergenerational knowledge. These conversations often entailed him imparting wisdom to me. The introduction of the tape recorder threatened, in my mind at least, to upend our respective roles and the rhythm we had developed. It also magnified two competing temporalities. I instrumentally desired—and needed—his words to complete my assignment; in contrast, he would usually share his stories when he felt it was appropriate for me to hear or learn from them, as a means of imparting wisdom. I worried that, even inadvertently, I was asking my grandfather to revisit experiences that he may have been hoping to leave in the past, espe-cially regarding the white supremacist anti-Filipinx violence and discrimin-ation he had endured.

I do not share this vignette to imply that I did not have enough dispas-sionate distance to research my own family. It was also not a matter of being more discreet in the placement of the tape recorder. The lesson I ultimately learned is that even in the most trusting of intimate relations, there are issues of power, responsibility, and appropriateness to consider in the gathering and co-production of data, and we thus need to be all the more ethically vigilant, transparent, and self-reflexive when researching alongside people from communities other than our own.

We (back to María Paula and Gerald) do not want to suggest that the knowledge passed down through communities is necessarily at odds with university-based research, or to imply that ethnographic research methods are, by definition, a form of colonial capture (the real colonial capture was the American occupation of and massacres in the Philippines, not the grand-child trying to unearth this buried history). Gerald and his grandfather did indeed return to the interview, and, through the interview protocol, Gerald was able to ask questions that might not otherwise have come up organically in their relationship. These include questions about their ancestral homeland in Mindanao, the experiences of the Manongs (a term for respected elders) of the 1920s–30s, and the creative strategies of survivance (Visanor, 2008) of a numerically small, colonized and racialized East Coast community in the first half of the 20th century—all topics which were not readily available (if at all) in the scholarly literature.

There were even possibilities for inquiry that were still unimaginable to Gerald at the time. For example, the interview might have been a first step in a community-wide effort to research the Filipinx experience in Queens, co-constructed with families and elders, as a means of reclaiming and recon-stituting local and subaltern histories of NYC. This could perhaps have been done in a manner that at once respected, fortified, and expanded existing relational bonds. But such a project would require culturally relevant and collaborative research design over time: much more than dropping into a context (even a very familiar one) with a tape recorder (or Zoom call, for that matter) and good intentions. Creating the conditions for this form of collective inquiry and epistemic interdependence is what we understand to be at the heart of CBRE.

These ethical considerations are ones that have been pointed out by community partners since the early stages of our partnership. María Hernández, a leader in the Mexican community who has been involved with the CARE Initiative since its inception, initially joined the collaboration as part of an intergenerational ESOL class. She cautioned that we do not ask the adult learners to share their life testimonials without any sense of how they may be used. This sentiment resonated with other families in the partnership, who voiced their negative experiences with university-based researchers. Families, in short, had felt used and objectified. Through her involvement with local immigrant rights and Latine organizations, María Hernández empowered herself to name this form of exploitation, not only by university researchers but also by others—including leaders of nonprofits, local aspiring politicians, and even city activists who claimed to speak "for the people."

María Hernández would eventually share her own testimonial at a keynote presentation at the Ethnography and Education Conference, but on her own terms and after significant dialogical engagement with members of the CARE Initiative over many years. She and all the community members were never in any way against research. Quite the opposite: They hold in great regard its potential to improve lives and make the world better. Many community members have in fact made significant personal sacrifices to gain access to scholarly opportunities for their families. What community members have taken issue with over the years is any form of epistemic objectification, where they are "theorized" rather recognized as theorists and intellectuals. Often there is even a double form of exploitation: Community members are objectified *and* their knowledge is often appropriated, lifted out of context, and circulated as a commodity or form capital by others.

What we believe is at the heart of the community members' concerns is a failure to acknowledge the importance of what indigenous scholars have termed "proper relations" (Smith, 2021) and feminist philosophers have conceptualized as an ethics of care (Collins, 2000). In research, as in life, we are in relation and mutually constituted by one another. Caring for one another, being concerned about others' flourishing while simultaneously acknowledging how others have shaped and edified our own selves, ought to be a primary methodological concern that drives collaborative inquiry. This does not imply that university-based researchers do not have expertise or that a doctoral student should not fulfill their assignments, such as analyzing a transcript from a community inquiry meeting for a methods course they are taking, if this is something participants support. Individuals have different roles in CBRE, and what is important is that we enact these roles ethically and in close consultation with others who are part of the work. This relational methodological approach is a collective form of what Gerald has characterized in previous work as systematic improvisation (Campano, 2007): where research design, data collection & interpretation, and dissemination of findings are not determined a priori by any one authoritative individual, but rather emerge organically from a creative alchemy of intellect and desire involving all members of the community of inquiry. The flowering of this relational and caring approach to research is eloquently expressed by María Hernández herself, who wrote the following in the comments section of a university-mandated research participant consent form:

Gracias por la ayuda, apoyo, cariño, tiempo y mucha enseñanza que nos brindan, he aprendido mucho de todas las experiencias que cada uno ha compartido. Ojalá esto pueda continuar por mucho tiempo porque todos necesitamos de todos y si continúa la comunicación podemos mejorar nuestro futuro y por supuesto dar mejor educación a nuestros hijos. Gracias.

[Thank you for the help, support, cariño (care/love), time, and much learning that you have given us. I learned a lot from all the experiences that each person has shared. Hopefully this can continue for a long time because we all need everyone and if the communication continues, we can improve our future and give a better education for our children. Thank you.]

Challenging Extractivist Methodologies

The doctoral students who have been involved in the CARE Initiative, as we have illustrated in Chapter 3, embrace an ethics of care and believe in the reciprocal and collaborative nature of knowledge production, which is time- and labor-intensive. And as much as we ourselves, as mentors, promote these values, we have found ourselves at cross-purposes with a more general zeitgeist in academia. Several students, for example, have felt the pressure to collect data and publish within the first few years of their graduate studies and to distinguish themselves early on in their programs. This pressure originates in part from the demands of a highly competitive job market, where the prospects for a secure livelihood in the professoriate become increasingly slim as many academic workers occupy precarious positions as adjuncts without livable wages, and the competition is perhaps exacerbated by social media where academics promote themselves and package their accomplishments. Early career mentoring programs sometimes reinforce a fairly aggressive and transactional approach to networking, publishing, and branding of one's academic identity as well. Even colleagues and administrators supportive of our work have cautioned our students to consider refraining from partnership research until they have tenure and are well established in the field. The worry is that with the tenure clock ticking, they may not get their research agenda off the ground to publish enough, or their research may be coded merely as service by reviewers. These neoliberal conditions, as many have argued, are increasingly shaping university-based knowledge production.

While the caution about partnering too early in one's career does speak to some of the realities of academia, we would suggest that perhaps these realities need to change. It is precisely during their graduate studies when new and emerging scholars ought to learn about developing ethical relationships with school districts, teachers, youth, neighborhood organizations, and community members. We know many examples of former doctoral students who have done so without compromising their abilities to publish significant research and navigate the demands of their respective academic positions. Universities also need to do more to support these long-term trusting relationships and the faculty who nurture these collaborations.

There have been significant positive steps in this direction. For example, several of Gerald's colleagues have worked to articulate a common understanding of community-engaged scholarship at the university so that it might be better recognized in promotion deliberations (Saltmarsh & Hartley, 2011). In our own disciplinary area of literacy, the mentoring program Cultivating New Voices among Scholars of Color (CNV), which exists under the auspices of the National Council for the Teachers of English (NCTE), consistently reinforces the message that we are first and foremost accountable to the communities we serve. And, in the broader field of education, prestigious foundations, such as Spencer and William T. Grant, have convened meetings on equity in research-practice partnerships, providing much-needed support and legitimacy to many who have been trying to do the difficult work of collaborating across pronounced institutional and social boundaries. If we don't present alternative methodologies to new generations of scholars, we risk reinforcing an extractivist approach to research, and, with it, transactional relationships with communities that are rooted in colonial and imperial histories.

In a 2022 article, the philosopher Linda Martin Alcoff characterizes what she terms extractivist epistemologies, an orientation to knowledge production which "treats both land and people primarily as resources" that can be extracted "from their political, ethical, and institutional context of articulation" (p. 5). We immediately call to mind the critiques of the elders of the CARE Initiative who refuse to indulge partnerships that are non-dialogical and where trust has not been developed and sustained over time. Drawing on two case studies, one concerning the biopiracy exploiting indigenous communities and the other about museums' collections of material artifacts and human remains, Alcoff provides a definition of extractivist epistemologies as having four features:

> the practice of ranking knowers, denying the need for collaboration across groups, defining values as non-relational and objectively determinable, and seeking exclusive appropriation and control over intellectual items such as knowledges and processes.
>
> (p. 16)

While Alcoff suggests correctives to these tendencies, we feel validated that the professional and ethical norms we had developed earlier in the CARE Initiative, in dialogue with community members, directly address extractivist epistemologies as well. This does not come as a surprise because our work has always been informed by feminist and decolonial epistemologists. But we are also drawn to these intellectual traditions because they resonate with what we have learned empirically from our community partners and their own concerns about ethical and just collaborations. We wanted to be explicit about the principles, to put them in writing, because as our partnership developed and more people were interested in becoming involved, we needed to ensure the collaboration would not become co-opted in a manner that is potentially exploitative of the individuals who had entrusted us to work alongside them and their families. The following norms were never meant to be exhaustive, and they are always open to revision and interpretation (see Campano, Ghiso, & Welch, 2015, for a more elaborated account of the norms and their inception). Nonetheless, they continue to serve as a conceptual touchstone for the CARE Initiative as we strive for horizontal relations.

Norm 1: Equality is the starting point not the end point
Norm 2: Community members' knowledge and perspectives must be taken seriously
Norm 3: Specific research foci and questions are co-designed with community members
Norm 4: Research should benefit the community
Norm 5: Research is made public in transparent, collaborative, and creative ways

Norm 1 speaks directly to the "practice of ranking knowers" (Alcoff, 2022), which is a product of coloniality and its mission of classifying and sorting humanity according to a linear notion of progress defined by a false universalization of Western European ideologies of modernity (Mignolo, 2011). This practice of ranking knowers through bell-curve ideologies is still constituent of our education system, manifested, for example, in the high-stakes testing paradigm and tracking, which reproduce inequalities along axes of race, class, and (dis)ability. The presumption of radical equality (Rancière, 2004) conveyed in Norm 1 entails viewing everyone as an intellectual, scholar, theorist, and researcher, irrespective of any aspects of their ascribed identities, such as their level of formal education. This norm exists in tension with the arrogance of the academy, which, too often, strives for a monopoly on knowledge production through acquisitive practices. The second norm promotes the value of collaborative thinking and multiperspectival approaches to inquiry. The norm requires epistemic humility, especially for those who hold relative positions of power and are affiliated with institutions that have an aura of authority, such as universities. The first two norms, we have found, are also essential for cultivating trusting relations. If members, or a member, of a research team do not feel as if they have something to learn from their partners, there can be very little genuine dialogue or foundation for collaboration.

Norms 3–5 help to ensure that the knowledge produced by CBRE does not become overly abstracted from the context and purposes of its production. No one person "owns" the research or has the final say on how it should be interpreted and used. The community members themselves formulate their own inquiries and are intimately involved in the processes by which knowledge is co-constructed, interpreted, and shared. While there can certainly be multiple knowledge projects involving different configurations of researchers, what is non-negotiable is that the research benefits the community by their own standards and values (Caine & Mill, 2016). This entails that the community researchers not only attend to issues of power in their own epistemic practices, but use their research to strike back at power, challenging dominant ideologies that pathologize youth and families by employing "non-relational" metrics that claim a false objectivity or universal value. CBRE is thus fueled by a type of situated, resistant intellectual struggle, a collective desire to mobilize research to right wrongs and prefigure more nourishing and liberatory educational possibilities.

We do not suggest that methodological approaches to research can be divided bluntly into extractive and non-extractive varieties, or that elements of extraction are necessarily problematic in every case. All research must be understood within its own contextual nuances and disciplinary histories and counter-histories, which will invariably be shaped by the conditions and institutions within which it arises. Our norms may serve as a reminder that educational research is governed by assumptions regarding how we view and engage others, and it is important for these assumptions to be made explicit, troubled, and revised. By articulating ethical and professional norms in our own iteration of CBRE, we hope to inspire others who are thinking through what it means to create horizontal knowledge projects, including university partnerships with schools, neighborhood centers, grassroots organizations, and faith communities. These local inquiries may collectively contribute to broader intellectual conversations that seek to (re)imagine education and research for a genuinely participatory and pluralistic democracy.

Building Horizontal Intellectual Relationships

CBRE is fueled by a network of relationships that aspire to become socially and intellectually non-hierarchical. It differs from more conventional hierarchical approaches to scholarship where the agenda is often driven by university-based researchers who, in a type of Platonic tradition, pursue the truth of participants educational lives, while the participants themselves may be positioned as unaware or not fully aware of their situations, as living "in the shadows" so to speak. For example, it is common for university-based researchers to develop metrics to assess and rank students' abilities through Eurocentric norms. Critical traditions in educational studies may also operate from a more hierarchical and transmission-based paradigm, where the goal might be for the university-researcher to expose how domination is reproduced through language and literacy practices, such as leveling, and then help to develop "critical consciousness" in participants around such issues (see critique by Ellsworth, 1989; Guerra, 2004). Even YPAR projects, with which CBRE overlaps and shares many affinities, may sustain intellectual hierarchies: Youth identify a problem and engage in a cycle of inquiry to investigate and act on the issue, but are often mentored by university faculty who may transmit to the youth the conceptual and methodological approaches of their academic fields and serve as a kind of intellectual and social role model for the youth to emulate.

In CBRE, university-based researchers certainly have important tools and expertise to contribute. But because it presumes all participants as always already researchers and intellectuals who cultivate their own critical perspectives, and it is the relationships themselves that drive the work together, CBRE may allow for more contingency, multiplicity, and unpredictability of inquiry than is typical of other methodological approaches. At any given period during the CARE Initiative, for example, there may be several projects occurring simultaneously: Parents may be engaging in action research on high school admissions, while a doctoral student and several youth are investigating the role of spirituality in education (LeBlanc, 2017), while we are trying to understand the nature of university-community partnerships, while the whole group is coming together to think about how communication between schools and families might be more transparent and dialogical.

Sometimes there is a lot going on and the partnership feels, to us, unwieldy and chaotic, yet energizing and rife with potential. Other times the work is more concentrated, involving the close collaboration of a few individuals. Some inquiries have a lot of initial momentum but lose energy. Other inquiries may germinate from a seemingly small observation by a community member and blossom into a full-blown research project. What may begin as primarily a pedagogical initiative, such as an ESOL class, may spontaneously transform into an inquiry about immigration or a reclaiming of buried histories and languages. For example, Emily Rose Schwab (2019), a member of the CARE Initiative, worked alongside her multilingual adult learners and employed dialogue journals to engage in reciprocal and collaborative research.. And, conversely, what may begin as an official action research project may become more of a teaching workshop, for example, on surveys—a skill which may, or may not, be picked up and utilized at a later point.

We believe this kind of flexibility and mutability to be a strength of CBRE. There are multiple rhizomatic entry points for individuals to (re)engage in the collaborative work, fostering inclusivity. The openness of the approach also allows for an improvisational sensibility, where participants may pursue previously unanticipated intellectual and desirous lines of flight. Because we are not beholden to a rigid or preset research agenda, the partnership can accommodate contingencies on different scales. Throughout the Covid pandemic we expanded our partnership to include youth beyond South Philadelphia through technology. We were also able to nurture existing relationships, inviting one another into our respective homes over Zoom, visiting on the front steps for exchanges of materials, food, or masks, and trying to comfort one another when life becomes especially difficult.

Of course, the contingency and unpredictability of CBRE does not come without its own challenges. Not everything that happens counts as research, and our work together needs to be intentional, systematic (if in an improvisational manner), and meaningful to the participants themselves as well as broader audiences. This requires a kind of planning that is perhaps best suited for those of us on the university-side of the partnership who have the luxury to meet regularly as part of our jobs. We have identified several tensions in our efforts to help organize a research community that strives for more horizontal social and intellectual relationships.

The first tension involves stabilizing the ongoing flux of potentiality in order to focus on something concrete without overly controlling or dictating the research agenda. This involves always analyzing the processes, not merely the products, of the partnership. Doctoral students and Youth Research Fellows take regular fieldnotes on our meetings and the time spent alongside community members, and we ourselves convene weekly as a university team to share any insights, patterns, or critical incidents as a form of collective listening. For example, we may notice that the community researchers raise a particular topic consistently that we have not paid enough attention to or acted on. Or we may hear that a particular protocol or activity that has become ritualized is no longer really working well for everyone, spurring a change or shift in direction. Data from the partnership is not used to narrowly interpret or characterize "participants," but to listen for perspectives we may have not noticed in the moment (Yoon & Templeton, 2019) and (re)consider our practices of partnering. We, on the university-side of the partnership, need to be self-reflexive about our own power in driving the research, and there is a fine line between mobilizing our privilege and resources to keep things productively moving forward and unduly taking over. Regular communication is key for establishing an equilibrium that balances established practices with new directions for inquiry. What is ultimately most important is that whatever we do as a research group is of value to community members, deepens our understanding of educational equity and access, and advances the epistemic rights of everyone involved.

A second tension relates to the ideas and conceptual frameworks which inform our scholarship. Striving for less hierarchical intellectual relationships does not mean that those of us affiliated with the university ought to suspend all the ideas and frameworks that have become near and dear to our hearts. We all bring insights, points of view, and wisdom derived from our respective life experiences, whether inside or outside of formal schooling, and the rich diversity of perspectives is a strength of CBRE. What warrants caution, however, is the scholarly tendency to hastily superimpose a theoretical construct onto empirical phenomena, especially onto our relationships with others.

We have already invoked several Deleuzian tropes, and at the risk of violating what we just said about conceptual superimposition, it may be worth citing Deleuze's own words on empiricism. Deleuze writes (Deleuze & Parnet, 1977/2007):

> I have always felt that I am an empiricist, that is a pluralist. But what does this equivalence between empiricism and pluralism mean? ... The abstract does not explain, but must itself be explained; and the aim is not to rediscover the eternal or the universal, but to find the conditions under which something new is produced (creativeness).
>
> (p. vii)

What resonates with us is the idea that everyone in the partnership, individually and collectively, is encouraged to take an inquiry stance into their day-to-day experiences and the empirical realities of their lives to make sense of their conditions and create possibilities for themselves. Concepts, in this approach, are tools with which researchers can help imagine novel ways of living and being in community, which is especially important in an educational and social system that is oppressive. Researchers, therefore, not only use ideas to read the world but also create new worlds, which will in turn generate new ideas. There is a dialectic between the conceptual and empirical. We have noticed that doctoral students working with us have been especially excited about sharing with youth researchers theories that they are learning about in their own studies, and this is totally cool because often the youth themselves find these theories empowering. But all community members also bring with them concepts and critical practices they have inherited from their own subaltern cultural legacies which become potential ingredients for the intellectual chemistry of the group (Campano, Ghiso, & Sánchez, 2013). And, perhaps most importantly, we try to nurture the conditions for members of the CARE Initiative to cultivate their own perspectives out of this robust intellectual pluralism.

A final tension involves balancing the desires of individuals and the good of the larger group. In principle we believe everyone within the context of the CARE Initiative should be able to investigate the lines of inquiry they so desire, and for the most part this has not been a problem. But what happens when someone would like to pursue a potential research relationship with ideas or people that may be harmful to the larger group, for example ones that are racist, classist, homophobic, or bullying? There have been a few cases where we, as university-based researchers, have used our authority and privilege to step in and say no, we need to protect the larger community. The community elders and Youth Research Fellows have done so as well. Some situations are complex, with a lot of gray area, and what is required is more of an intervention and dialogue. Other times we have felt the need to act quickly and decisively. For all the tensions we have found there are no simple rules to determine how to move forward. Like so many things in life, they call for a sensitivity to the particularities of each situation and good judgment, especially when involving salient social differences around race, class, gender, immigration status, and disability.

Trust as the Foundation for CBRE

A requirement for successful partnerships is trust and a collective ethos. The elders in the CARE Initiative have played a special role in mentoring new incoming members (such as doctoral students) on how to work respectfully and thoughtfully with families. Daria Ward, a community elder who has been part of the partnership since the beginning, regularly opens up her home to university students and researchers and describes her understanding of hospitality and community: "Community is offering yourself, your home, your food, making people feel comfortable and just sitting down and having a conversation … And that's something I found with our group." These care practices serve multiple functions: they fortify relational bonds, are a collaborative method of inquiry literally akin to kitchen-table talk (Lyiscott et al., 2021), and create opportunities for mentoring into the ethics of research. One former graduate student recounted how the lunch gatherings with Daria helped illuminate community perspectives on the partnership:

> [I]n retrospect I feel like she was teaching me how to do research—she said, in the candid way she does, "Nobody cares how many degrees you have after your name, what they care about is that you're a nice person and that you're a person that they can trust."

During these informal lunch conversations, issues of educational equity arise organically, including making explicit what it means to embody a non-extractive stance toward research. These discussions of research ethics are ones that other elders have conveyed over a cafecito with different individuals or while working side-by-side on arts projects, cultural events, and even room clean-ups after meetings. Learning about and helping address the issues facing communities has not been gleaned solely through tools such as surveys or interviews, but dialogically co-constructed over time through relationships of mutual respect that many in the group characterize as genuine friendship.

A relational approach to research is difficult emotional work. While long-term relationships can help members of a partnership give each other the benefit of the doubt when challenges arise, there is also greater potential for hurt because of the deeper level of investment people have in one another's lives. Missteps can result in a betrayal of trust. For instance, we had a recent situation when inadvertently excluding some members from an event—regardless of the factors that led to this—could have upended our partnership. After the peak of Covid had subsided, we thought it would be helpful to meet with the CARE elders in person to discuss how to move the project forward, especially since many in the partnership had endured loss. We were also experiencing changes on the university-side of the team, as graduating doctoral students cycled out of the project and newer ones took on leadership roles. These various shifts led to a mistake where a family who had previously been involved with the partnership was not invited to our dinner meeting while an invite was extended to a potential new collaborator. As soon as we sat down, one of the leaders from the Latine community asked María Paula directly about this exclusion; she was absolutely right in raising this omission, and we were mortified. More than about missing a meeting, this oversight could have conveyed a devaluing of the family's involvement, in the process also undermining the group as a whole. The thicker relationships in CBRE raise the stakes of trust and give greater weight to our actions. Seemingly small missteps can signify a betrayal. We left the dinner and immediately contacted the mother to express our heartfelt apologies and made sure to prioritize her schedule in planning a partnership event a few weeks after. Mistakes are bound to happen. What we have learned is the importance of addressing breaches of trust swiftly and directly, acknowledging harms, and working to repair the relationship in order to move forward. Academia has many restrictive gatherings and societies, but as a general rule these kinds of exclusionary practices have no place in CBRE. A sense of belonging is crucial.

Methodology as a Practice of Love

There is a more ineffable aspect of cultivating and nurturing the relational bonds necessary for CBRE. One of the advantages of the participatory documentary that Dee created of the CARE Initiative, which assembles footage and images from close to ten years of the project (see Chapter 7 for a description of this process), is that we were able to watch interactions that we may have taken for granted. The film was able to convey better than other forms of representation, such as a scholarly article, the affective dimensions of our work. There are scenes, for example, of individuals expressing bonds of care and solidarity through hugging, shedding tears, laughing, and even dancing. Watching the film, we realize that the group has woven together a common past. This past is what makes the relationships in the CARE Initiative more than instrumentally directed toward individuals' future goals. The group is building a legacy together.

   Whenever we watch the film, we relive moments of the project when many in the group felt a sense of awe derived from being part of something greater than individual selves. One example occurred during a poignant and powerful presentation at the 2018 Annual Meeting of the American Educational Research Association in New York City, when the families assembled the hallways of the conference center because their assigned presentation room was too small to contain the crowd. The respondent, Dr. Yolanda Sealey-Ruiz, delivered an eloquent synthesis of the presentations and many of the family members expressed validation that their research, and by implication their dehumanizing experiences with schooling, was truly heard and understood.

   These moments remind us that nourishing the relational bonds for CBRE is not simply a cognitive exercise or a matter of adhering to specific norms. Not only do we, as a research community, think alongside one another; we *feel* alongside one another as well. As Audre Lorde (1978) has theorized, "The sharing of joy, whether physical, emotional, psychic, or intellectual, forms a bridge between the sharers which can be the basis for understanding much of what is not shared between them, and lessens the threat of their difference" (p. 7).

   The emotion that best captures the affective dimension of CBRE is love. It is ultimately love which breaks down the subject-object dichotomy that structures extractivist epistemologies, nurturing what Buber (1923/2013) characterizes as I-Thou (subject-subject) rather than I-It, (subject-object) relationships. It has been the elders in our project who have taught us about the kind of love required in CBRE to bridge differences. Daria, for example, has stated that one's heart "needs to be big enough for all communities, not just one community." Others have discussed the ways we are all interconnected, no matter where we are from. These insights resonate with the thoughts of the political philosopher Michael Hardt (2007), who has discussed, primarily in interviews, the role of love in social justice movements, from Gandhi to King. It is a love which embraces multiplicity and difference; not an exclusive love of the same or the assimilable, which in fact is a corruption of love that can too easily become weaponized to homogenize difference, stoke hate, and scapegoat others. Real love, by contrast, makes more porous the boundaries between self and other, but it does not collapse self and other, as in the western stereotype of romantic love. We presume that none of our experiences can be contained by the ascribed categories and rankings too often used to define us. At the same time, we leave ourselves open to learn from and be transfigured by others, especially by those who have more acutely experienced the inequities of our shared social world. It is also love which compels us to view each individual in the project, and beyond the project, as sacred and precious.

Although many may find the emphasis on love in scholarship sentimental, we are heirs to a legacy of embracing love in pedagogy, not merely as a feeling but also as a practice of resistance to oppressive structures (Biana, 2021), going back to hooks (2000) and Freire (1970). We extend this legacy in pedagogy to research methodology as well. Although there is much left to understand about the relationship between love and research, the whole of this book is one initial and modest attempt to express how we have imagined and understood Community-Based Research in Education as a methodology and practice of love. Love remains our North Star for understanding how research might inform and prefigure a more just education for all.

Questions for Reflection

1. How might you cultivate a research ethos that challenges extractivist epistemologies?
2. What ethical and professional norms guide your own work? How will you negotiate challenging situations and foster good judgment?
3. What role do affect and emotion play in your research?

References

Alcoff, L. M. (2022). Extractivist epistemologies. *Tapuya: Latin American Science, Technology and Society, 5*(1), 2127231.

Biana, H. T. (2021). Love as an act of resistance: Bell hooks on love. In S. Hongladarom & J. J. Joaquin (Eds.), *Love and friendship across cultures: Perspectives from East and West* (pp. 27–137). Springer.

Buber, M. (2013). *I and thou* (R. G. Smith, Trans.). Bloomsbury. (Original work published 1923.)

Caine, V., & Mill, J. (2016). *Essentials of community-based research*. Routledge.

Campano, G. (2007). *Immigrant students and literacy: Reading, writing, and remembering*. Teachers College Press.

Campano, G., Ghiso, M. P., & Sánchez, L. (2013). "No one knows the…amount of a person": Elementary students critiquing dehumanization through organic critical literacies. *Research in the Teaching of English, 48*(1), 98–125.

Campano, G., Ghiso, M. P., & Welch, B. (2015). Ethical and professional norms in community-based research. *Harvard Educational Review, 85*(1), 29–49.

Collins, P. H. (2000). *Black feminist thought: Knowledge, consciousness, and the politics of empowerment* (2nd ed.). Routledge.

Deleuze, G., & Parnet, C. (2007). *Dialogues II: Revised edition* (H. Tomlinson & B. Habberjam, Trans.). Columbia University Press. (Original work published 1977.)

Ellsworth, E. (1989). Why doesn't this feel empowering? Working through the repressive myths of critical pedagogy. *Harvard Educational Review, 59*(3), 297–325.

Freire, P. (1970). *Pedagogy of the oppressed*. Continuum.

Guerra, J. (2004). Putting literacy in its place: Nomadic consciousness and the practice of transcultural repositioning. In C. Gutiérrez-Jones (Ed.), *Rebellious reading: The dynamics of Chicana/o cultural literacy* (pp. 19–37). University of California, Santa Barbara, Chicano Studies Institute.

Hardt, M. (2007, June 25). About love [Video]. European Graduate School Video Lectures. YouTube. www.youtube.com/watch?v=ndnkjnMxxLc

hooks, b. (2000). *All about love: New visions*. William Morrow.

Immerwahr, D. (2019). *How to hide an empire: A history of the greater United States*. Farrar, Straus and Giroux.

LeBlanc, R. J. (2017). Literacy rituals in the community and the classroom. *Language Arts, 95*(2), 77–86.

Lorde, A. (1978). *Uses of the erotic: The erotic as power*. Out & Out Books.

Lyiscott, J., Green, K., Ohito, E., & Coles, J. (2021). Call us by our names: A kitchen table dialogue on doin' it for the culture. *Equity & Excellence in Education, 54*(1), 1–18.

Mignolo, W. (2011). I am where I think: Remapping the order of knowing. In F. Lionnet & S. Shih (Eds.), *The creolization of theory* (pp. 159–192). Duke University Press.

Rancière, J. (2004). *The philosopher and his poor*. Duke University Press.

Saltmarsh, J., & Hartley, M. (Eds.). (2011). *"To serve a larger purpose": Engagement for democracy and the transformation of higher education*. Temple University Press.

Schwab, E. R. (2019). Writing together: Reclaiming dialogue journals as a mutually humanizing teaching practice. *Literacy Research: Theory, Method, and Practice, 68*(1), 108–129.

Smith, L. T. (2021). *Decolonizing methodologies: Research and indigenous people* (3rd ed.). Bloomsbury.

Visanor, G. (Ed.). (2008). *Survivance: Narratives of native presence*. University of Nebraska Press.

Yoon, H., & Templeton, T. N. (2019). The practice of listening to children: The challenges of hearing children out in an adult-regulated world. *Harvard Educational Review, 89*(1), 55–84.

5 How Do You Develop and Support Collaboration?

Consensus Building in CBRE

The relationship between schools and families is a topic of prominent concern for the CARE Initiative and has shaped many of our inquiries. While there seems to be a consensus in the education field that parents and families play an important role in their children's schooling, how educational institutions might better learn from them and overcome longstanding barriers to trust and communication derived from histories of racial subordination remains an ongoing question. There have been many top-down initiatives to foster family "engagement" and "participation," but these efforts often fall short of genuine epistemic and social cooperation. They also often assume a white middle-class conception of parental school involvement (e.g., Lopez, 2009). At the same time, there are increasing calls for university-based researchers to conduct research alongside community members, but it is not always clear what this looks like as a day-to-day practice. In this chapter we strive to demystify the process of bridging the divides between educational institutions and communities through collaborative inquiry. We describe the collaborative practices we have developed over the years with the idea that they may be applicable to many partnerships in a variety of contexts. We ourselves continue to draw from them as the CARE Initiative strives to involve more teachers and school leaders, a key goal of the families.

Throughout our work together, we have investigated how a commitment to research that is driven by the intellectual contributions of families, youth, and community leaders can be built into the workings of our partnership. How do groups undertaking community-based research translate big-picture principles into ways of interacting with one another? How do the structures of the research collaboration support its aims of participatory justice? How can partnership practices remain attentive to equity and not reinscribe the power differentials they are seeking to disrupt? Cox (2021) argues that the redistribution of power in organizations occurs through the dialectic of individual interactions and broader structures that support horizontal relationships and decision-making. We find this dual lens helpful because it underscores how individual actions and collective practices work in concert to create the

DOI: 10.4324/9781003279686-5

conditions for genuine and meaningful collaborative work. While Cox focuses on institutional efforts, we would add that change is also driven from the ground up, by communities themselves exercising their power, interrogating hierarchies and unequal practices, and demanding more just arrangements that honor their full human dignity.

In this chapter, we discuss practices that support the co-construction of research directions. Some of these have developed into formalized routines or structures (such as goal-setting meetings to begin the year or paid Research Fellow roles for youth) and others are more informal habits and ways of being with one another that foster care, trust, and shared epistemic authority. The practices are both a starting point for collaborative work and a touchstone to revisit and sustain CBRE. They aid in the ongoing process of reflection and refinement, generating new ways of working together as collaborations evolve and deepen. In the sections that follow, we unpack illustrative moments from our partnership to think through possible practices for determining research directions, reflecting on accomplishments, and responding to the circumstances of precarity that impact individuals, groups, and institutions. We also discuss how these practices might be reimagined to foreground shared authority and complex communication (Lugones, 2006; Medina, 2020).

Collectively Determining Research Directions

Part of being a scholar is making an argument for a specific program of research, and one need only look at a sampling of handbooks or dissertation guides to notice how framings of "the problem" that a study seeks to address overwhelmingly originate in the literature and are then applied to research contexts. CBRE challenges the unidirectionality of this design, and necessitates thinking about the interplay between the body of scholarship within a discipline and the perspectives and goals of research partners. Community members, because of their lived struggles, are often attuned to issues of equity that the academy is less aware of, and therefore may anticipate cutting-edge and urgent areas of study. New directions may emerge from the synergy between university-based researchers and communities, including parents, youth, teachers, educational leaders, and local organizations.

In the CARE Initiative, we have intentionally created opportunities to think together about research directions. We begin each inquiry cycle with a whole group gathering to (re)connect, revisit prior understandings, and set the agenda for the coming year. We also have standing meetings at the midpoint and end of the year, informal check-ins that happen individually via preferred modes of communication (such as WhatsApp, Instagram, or phone calls), and built-in opportunities for reflection and goal setting, such as at the culmination of youth group meetings or during our weekly planning sessions. While some ideas are raised explicitly during dedicated times for co-design, others percolate more slowly or may be shared spontaneously during individual exchanges or as new issues organically arise. Our collective priorities may shift or there may be a need to adjust or change course, which can only be discerned and addressed through ongoing dialogue. Like other core tenets in CBRE, co-constructing research directions is not a one-time event, but an ongoing process.

Leading with Community Questions

A key feature of any research is the questions it is seeking to answer. CBRE is centered on the questions communities *themselves* have about educational justice. This framing, by its very nature, challenges research hierarchies and repositions families as leaders in research. The CARE Initiative has been grounded in iterative opportunities to surface communities' priorities and questions—even questions about whether to have a partnership at all. Our relationship began with individual leaders, who introduced us to the greater parish population and their existing organizational structure of a council that brought together representatives of the various cultural and linguistic groups on a monthly basis. The lead priest at the time helped us to craft an agenda for discussing a possible collaboration. To maximize participation, the session was structured as a combination of concurrent conversations in language affinity groups (Spanish, English, Vietnamese, and Indonesian) and whole group conversations with translations.

The meeting, as reflected in notes taken by the priest (see Figure 5.1), surfaced a range of issues and questions which over the years were shaped into various research designs. For example, a recurring theme of wanting to understand the processes of high school or college admissions, perhaps via workshops or other programming, later evolved into an action research project with Indonesian families (Yee, Mostafa, & Campano, 2016) and a college access inquiry (Campano et al., 2016; Ghiso et al., 2022). The families and community leaders also prioritized cultural maintenance and revitalization and the influence of sociopolitical factors in students' educational opportunities (e.g., jobs, housing, and immigration status).

Meeting attendees also had questions regarding the partnership with the university. One was a "General question regarding the university: Who are they? What role can they play? What happens next?", a comment which challenges the idea of partnerships as an assumed good. There was also a commitment to "continuing/free exchange" that would entail "shar[ing]" and "be[ing] critical." That is, any research design would necessarily involve a bidirectional flow of ideas that encourages constructive feedback. Over more than a decade, we have worked closely with many different members of the parish community, including a number of elders present at this initial meeting, and extended our networks to other families, youth, and community leaders.

Brainstorming
7 April 2011

Latino community
   Children
   o Tutoring/homework help
   o Story/reading time
   Youth
   o Community service hours – adult supervision
   o College support
   o Cultural awareness – language/culture
   Family
   o ESL/GED and advanced
   o Parenting: how to support children; navigating schools
   o Women's group – eg., conflict resolution
   o Connecting to resources already in community: cooking, medical, legal
   o Retreats have been successful – need for follow-up

Indonesian community
   Children: need Sat/Sun programs for 11-15 year olds
   Youth
   o Art/sport/games/video – what kids want
   o Activities for girls
   Family
   o Info regarding higher education (college/university): tests/interviews, application
      process, funding (scholarships)

Vietnamese community
   Children
   o Workshop/classes – language/culture
   o Homework help – tutoring
   Youth
   o ESL classes – lots of recent arrivals (10-22)
   o American culture – holidays, customs, food, culture
   o College – application process, funding
   o Bringing youth of different cultures together
   Family
   o ESL classes
   o Translators – medical/legal
   o Workshop on bridging cultures – parent/child (adolescent)
   o Workshop on school system/choices and higher education – college application
      process, finances
   General question regarding university: Who are they? What role can they play? What
   happens next?

Figure 5.1 Notes from initial research collaboration meeting.

English speaking communities (Italian-American, African-American, Filipino)
Children
  o Cultural/academic enrichment
  o Stretching beyond school to family – language and culture
Youth
    o ESL/GED
    o Monthly inter-cultural journal published by youth
    o Youth event
    o Career day
    o Exposure to college campus/students (especially first generation of their own culture)
    o Youth leadership
Family
    o ESL – but also American culture – integration
    o Honoring culture of each community

Floor open for comments
monthly intercultural student journal
citizenship – support for those going through process
free legal help (paralegal) for those going through immigration process
multicultural night: food, cultural traditions
continuing free exchange: share, be critical
job placement/fair
looking at needs that affect the community: jobs, housing, etc.
summer or after school jobs for youth: working on this project

Next steps
Immediate: Family night – story time for kids; workshop on reading for parents
Summer: Activities for youth
    o Possible small stipend for involvement
    o Across communities and age groups
    o Reading camp/club
    o Do some brainstorming with youth leaders
    o Park – cook-out

Figure 5.1 (Continued)

Logistics as An Opportunity to Enact Equity Commitments

Planning for collective goal setting is more than "busy-work"—it is an opportunity to address power dynamics and materialize principles of shared authority. Researchers might think about, for example, who is involved in the planning, how the agenda is decided upon and facilitated, where and when events will take place, and what outside factors might need to be taken into account to support participation (e.g., childcare, transportation, language, work schedules). These considerations have no ready-made answers. They may differ from project to project or across the span of a research partnership. For example, we have alternated between community sites and university spaces to underscore how research moves across these contexts. At one year's opening session, when there were a number of new members of the CARE Initiative, we highlighted the cultural, civic, and activist landscape of the neighborhood, discussing critical issues and situating our research in relation to existing community organizing efforts (see Ghiso et al., 2019). We visited important neighborhood locations and, with input from community leaders, prepared information sheets on them with a list of questions for reflection and analysis. These sites included several schools, a health clinic, a new library, two businesses that reflect neighborhood gentrification, and a local park that was part of the civil rights movement and which continues to be a vibrant gathering place. Through the activity, we were able to prioritize and learn from community perspectives of the neighborhood and frame the research goals we would subsequently craft together within a broader social context.

We have also met at the university to create space for families who have been excluded from its borders. While many families from affluent areas have ready-made access to the campus and faculty members' children (including our daughter) grow up with a sense that the university is part of their backyard, others may live in proximity to the campus but are made to feel as if they do not belong there (Campano et al., 2016). Facilitating campus access has been one way to promote a reciprocal partnership. Even decisions such as where to purchase food send a message. When possible, we have tried to support community-owned businesses and establishments from the neighborhoods in which members of our research partnership live. These considerations require extra time and sometimes cause friction with university bureaucracies, which have well-defined channels for existing vendors and corporate relationships but less so with regards to community establishments.

While co-planning sessions is an essential part of determining research directions, we are also mindful of being an imposition to families, educators, and community leaders with already full schedules, demanding work, and caregiving responsibilities. University-researchers may need to make decisions about when participation in co-planning may be most feasible for and desired by community partners, as well as think creatively about the different forms of involvement. Can larger goals be discussed together, and then a tentative plan drafted and shared with community members for revision? Can there be outreach to different constituents in the pre-planning stages? Might different individuals alternate planning and/or facilitation of meetings? Are there ways to refer back to the desires of co-researchers who may not be present during planning sessions? Incorporating reflection across all research gatherings and activities—such as taking time to discuss what practices worked or didn't, or what changes we would like to see in our ways of working together at the end of sessions—can help ensure that all major issues are on the table when not everyone can be in the room crafting the agenda.

Responding to Precarity and Changing Circumstances

Even as processes are developed to establish modes of co-constructing research, these need to be adapted or revisited in response to changing circumstances. Though it may seem obvious that what worked at one point will not necessarily continue to work, the reality is that we may all develop attachments to our usual ways of doing things. This goes just as much for collective processes created through partnership efforts and community priorities as for normative academic routines. Over the years our group has refined forms of communication, ways of disseminating information, and preferred meeting times among various partnership members. Given how much there is to negotiate in CBRE, these practices have become a sort of "short cut" for organizing meetings, research, and events. At the same time, being responsive to the circumstances of everyone in our research community has entailed flexibility, going back to the drawing board and taking on new challenges as we support one another.

For example, our partnership has usually met on weekends because that is a time when families and youth have been available. Yet with the economic downturn elders have had to take on additional jobs, and many work in the service industry where weekends are the busiest periods. As youth have grown older and accrued additional responsibilities, whether in schooling or work, their schedules have also become harder to coordinate. In addition, the community space where we had typically held our meetings underwent a leadership transition and Covid-shutdown, and as a result the usual patterns of gathering became disrupted. During such periods of change, we touch base with everyone individually to see what they are going through, how the partnership may be able to support them, and how research practices should shift to accommodate new realities. This may mean that some collective work happens asynchronously, as smaller groups meet when possible and one-on-one talks become opportunities to elicit feedback that can then be shared with the larger group. There may be fewer gatherings with the entire research collective, with phone calls, Zoom gatherings, social media or text chats, and walks in the neighborhood taking on greater importance in joint planning.

These solutions involve more time, facilitation, and recursive sharing among various members of the group, bumping up against expectations of "efficiency" and productivity that permeate both academic cultures as well as Pk-12 educational institutions. As with any research, individuals involved in CBRE may all experience changing circumstances that impact their ability to be involved. We view what many research paradigms may characterize as "attrition," or a typical loss of study participants over time, as an opportunity to think about how the work is being carried out and what would enhance community participation.

CBRE aspires to create research communities of care and reciprocity. Our responsibilities to each other extend beyond a particular research protocol as we are attentive to and seek to support each other through life challenges, which are exacerbated by the social inequalities. Infirmity, mental health and wellness, economic instability, family loss, displacement, and incarceration are all material realities that have impacted members of the CARE Initiative, and they are not external to CBRE. First and foremost, there is a need to be aware of what people are going through, including understanding their desires to step away from the research for as little or as long as they decide, and communicating that they are always welcome to return. Challenges that community members are experiencing may, in time, become new areas of inquiry and action which the partnership undertakes. These new research priorities often unsettle the academic silos because people's lives, and the inequities they face and seek to change, do not conform to codified disciplinary boundaries. University-based researchers may need to stretch beyond their intellectual comfort zones to be responsive to community members' lives as whole human beings.

Moving Forward: Balancing Reflection and Action

One ongoing consideration in CBRE is how to balance the need for community-driven, iterative co-design without imposing on individuals who have other competing responsibilities and constraints in their lives. We want to make sure that research is respectful of and guided by communities' own goals for educational equity (reflection) while at the same time be mindful that enacting such respect also requires action (moving things forward). Partnership norms and practices can help in setting expectations and "next steps" for check-ins and progress toward shared research.

A recent CBRE initiative offers an illustrative example. A recurring and longstanding theme from families, youth, and community leaders has been the intersection between education and other issues of equity in the city, such as gentrification and the erosion of neighborhood schools (Campano et al., 2022). One of the youth researchers, a photographer and visual artist who has been interested in arts-based pedagogies as a form of educational justice, proposed a new research project: to utilize photovoice as a means of documenting the cultural vibrancy and resistance of the city's Chinatown residents currently fighting a proposed sports stadium that threatens to upend the neighborhood. This new line of inquiry would involve CARE Initiative youth as well as youth from the Chinatown neighborhood.

Before undertaking this research, we wanted to meet with community leaders who were involved in the organizing efforts, including a director from a local Asian American organization, an activist and elder who has been involved in the Chinatown community, and a teacher who was raised in Chinatown and whose family still resides there. All these individuals have contributed to the CARE Initiative over the years, and we convened them as an advisory group with specialized knowledge for undertaking this youth-proposed research. When we met with the advisors, it became clear that we, on the university-side of the partnership, were so worried about imposing a research agenda that we came across as vague about the goals of the project

Figure 5.2 Flyer for youth inquiry planning meeting.

and how it might contribute to the larger organizing efforts. The community leaders, by contrast, raised pointed questions about what the project would entail, how it would benefit youth, and how participants would know that this was a worthwhile undertaking. They wanted to know, in short, how the research would be useful. Their advice shaped the next stage of the project and was incorporated into a flyer advertising a planning meeting (Figure 5.2), where the design of the research (data collection, inquiry sessions, analysis, etc.) would be determined alongside youth and neighborhood representatives.

Pedagogies for Collective Decision-Making

We have found CBRE has a strong pedagogical dimension. Educational researchers may draw on their own experiences as teachers in considering how to organize opportunities for the inquiry community to think and plan together. Strategies for facilitation may also tap into the organizing experiences of youth, families, and local leaders. For example, a number of CARE members are well versed in techniques to support consensus building through youth empowerment and leadership programming and other forms of grassroots public pedagogy. They have experience, for example, in drawing on community funds of knowledge (González et al., 2006), facilitating difficult conversations, speaking truth to power, and mobilizing formal and informal networks to advocate for change. Their expertise has helped our partnership make collective decisions about the direction of our research.

We offer the extended planning notes in Figure 5.3 to illustrate our decision-making and consensus-building process. The late summer or early fall, when this session took place, is a recurring time when we gather together to revisit priorities and co-construct the year ahead. During the meeting, we returned to a community-generated list of demands for educational equity, distilled as a result of synthesizing themes from our research several years into the partnership, which has been a guiding document (see Chapter 6 for details on its origins). Consensus building focused on two areas: (1) prioritizing three themes from the broader research agenda of the demands to focus on during the coming year; (2) thinking through how these themes could be taken up directly with educators. The practices we describe below, though specifically referencing this meeting agenda, are utilized in many of our gatherings.

The CARE team made intentional decisions to facilitate consensus building:

- *Allocating Extended Time.* Collective goal setting cannot be rushed, and a longer meeting time enables different perspectives to be heard and options to be discussed more fully. In our example, the session lasted 3 hours, allowing for a range of interactive activities.
- *Strengthening Relational Bonds.* Spending time on relationships and deepening trust is the foundation for undertaking joint projects—the key to navigating difficult topics thoughtfully and with critical generosity toward one another. Time to eat and socialize at the beginning of meetings allows people to come in on their schedules, especially as many may be transitioning from other responsibilities or traveling via public transportation. We often use this "trickle in time" to check in about upcoming events, gather needed information (such as preferred modes of contact, in the case of our sample agenda), and solicit input. It is also when members of a research collective can be present for and learn about each other. We have found that informal times spent congregating are when community partners might offer their perspectives one-on-one, share ideas, and raise concerns. These insights may, over time, materialize into a more formal research agenda.
- *Diversifying Forms of Participation.* Creating multiple and differing opportunities for discussion is essential. We pay special attention to how varying practices and configurations might mitigate power dynamics and support all members in contributing their thoughts. In our example, we created

Goals of this Session:
- Reconnect
- Establish overview of the year
- Generate ideas for inquiries utilizing previously determined demands
- Build tentative focus areas for professional development with teachers

Activities:
1. Food and Activity Set Up - 12:30-1:00
2. 1:00-1:45 (Eat food and **connect**)
   a. Trickle-in: Get updated contact information from youth and parents
3. 1:45-2:10 PM (Welcome Back, sharing out from doctoral student pilot studies, introduction of Dee and Ankhi share out their pilot projects and introduce the PD idea)
4. 2:10-2:20: Elders from the partnership talk about the history of the demands.
5. 2:20-2:50: SMALL GROUP EXPERT GROUP
   a. Small Group activity (Designated members of the research team sit at each table and take notes of the discussion. These are a mix of experienced youth researchers, graduate students, and Co-PIs):
      i. Which of the demands resonates the most with you and why? Tell a story to your table that shows why it resonates with you.
      ii. What are other priorities that this professional development should cover that is not included in the demands?
6. 2:50-3:15- SMALL GROUP JIGSAW
   a. Number off each member of your group (1-5 for example)
   b. Have people switch groups so there is representation from each of the original group in new groups.
   c. Share some of the most important stories and ideas that came from your group
   d. As a group, discuss some of the important overlaps between demands and other priorities. Make a list in the group of what the professional development should prioritize (3 Things)
   e. **Share out whole group your 3 things and why they are so important**
      i. Facilitator PLEASE WRITE THESE DOWN ON CHART PAPER
7. 3:10-3:40- Priority Activity- Whole Group Share-Out and Activity
   a. Explain that as a community, we need to hone in on focus areas.
   b. Explain that each person will have 5 votes. Put a dash next to the priority that you feel is important. You can give all your votes to 1 priority OR distribute them among various.
   c. Give time for the facilitator to tally up votes with the group.
   d. **Announce the priorities (Fellows)**
8. 3:40: 4:00: Closing
   a. Whole-Group Reflection
      i. What did you learn?
      ii. What resonated with you?
      iii. What ideas do you have for next steps to move the PD development process forward?
   b. Announce next youth meeting
   c. Group Picture :)
   d. Take food home and clean-up

Figure 5.3 Meeting plans for setting the year's collective research agenda.

two opportunities for group conversations following a jigsaw format. First individuals discussed stories from their lives or communities that exemplified a particular educational demand they considered important, such that each group deepened their understanding of intersecting issues

impacting educational equity. In a second round of discussions, individuals represented the ideas formed in their respective groups to glean
patterns and gain a collective understanding of how and why these issues
mattered to the larger partnership. The decision about how to structure the
groups is a choice of the research community as a whole, but might be
informed by the preferred language of individuals (one group was run in
Spanish, the others in English), existing cultural practices that may facilitate discussion (such as storytelling and testimonio as a form of research),
considerations regarding translation, and expertise on multiple modes of
conveying meaning, such as art.

- *Designating Facilitation Roles.* Having pre-established facilitators helps to
tack back-and-forth between small group and whole group discussions
and to gather different perspectives. The facilitators might rotate across
meetings and represent the different sub-communities within the partnership. Meeting planners ought to be thoughtful about how roles are
decided upon or assigned, whether perspectives are being left out, and
how opportunities for facilitation can be modified. In this example,
facilitators included ourselves as university faculty, graduate students, and
youth researchers who had helped co-plan that day's meeting. We had also
met prior to this event to agree on what facilitation would entail, such as
ensuring everyone gets a chance to speak and aiding with documentation
(charting, etc.) to make insights visible to the whole group.

- *Taking Action.* As much as deliberation is important, is it also necessary to
move beyond discussion to arrive at decisions together. This imperative does
not imply that deliberation be curtailed at the expense of decision-making,
but that each group considers how to balance discussion and action steps.
In the case of the agenda in Figure 5.3, after hearing from everyone in the
research collective, participants were asked to vote for their top priorities to
pursue in the coming year, whether by deciding on one specific point they
wanted to advocate for or distributing their votes across a range of options.
This prioritizing and goal setting did not preclude returning to other ideas at
a later point or adjusting course as necessary, but it did allow the group to
take action through a collectively agreed-upon process.

- *Prioritizing Transparency.* Transparency is a precondition for equitable
partnerships and must be threaded throughout all aspects of the research
process. In setting collective agendas, this can include transparency about
how research questions are decided, the constraints of or incentives for
employing a particular method, and the end goals of the research. In
our sample meeting agenda, we began with transparency about ongoing
research. Doctoral students who had conducted pilot studies with youth
from the partnership presented on their projects, including how they
were interpreting the data collected. The pilot projects had been previously approved and discussed with the research collective, but this was
an opportunity, to revisit those conversations and learn about any new
developments. In cases where university-based researchers might take the

lead on something institutionally (such as, for example, IRB protocols or a grant application), we explain the rationale for doing so, as well as invite input and critique. We were also transparent about the purpose and process of the goal-setting meeting. In the meeting, community elders spoke about the history of the partnership and how we arrived collectively at the educational demands. What is implicitly expressed throughout the whole agenda is that the research belongs to our entire community and not just to the university representatives.

As researchers engage in the co-design of practices that can guide CBRE, one non-negotiable starting point is to make the collaborative process as inclusive as possible. This may entail questioning assumptions about taken-for granted ways of working and thinking through solutions to barriers that may arise. We might reflect on, for example, whether certain individuals become stand-ins for community participation and whether roles and communication channels are reproducing existing hierarchies. What will it take to elicit a broader range of perspectives? How might CBRE partnerships engage multiple viewpoints and linger in discussion while still progressing in action? What are the tensions or conflicts in making research decisions, and how might these be productively resolved?

In our partnership, for example, there are language differences among the respective cultural communities, and our meetings have evolved over time to displace monolingualism as the norm. One interactional feature of our meetings has been that individuals who are bilingual take it upon themselves to translate when needed, whether in whole group discussions, side conversations, or by conducting small group breakouts by language. At the same time, everyone is also accustomed to the fact that they will not understand everything that is said, that each of us will need to become comfortable with this linguistic pluralism. These types of meetings, which strive for multilingual inclusion, require a longer time commitment, with people waiting patiently as ideas are translated to the entire group. By decoupling linguistic proficiency from intellectual contributions in our everyday ways of engaging with one another, these moment-to-moment interactions prefigure the types of horizontal relationships that are central to CBRE.

Building Consensus Through Difference

As the co-construction of CARE research directions indicates, the impetus for the educational research conducted by the families is to improve schooling. Families have cogent firsthand knowledge and insights to share, but schools are not typically set up to learn from them (Ishimaru, 2019). Our partnership decided that one lever for change is to infuse community research into professional development opportunities for educators. Too often, the training teachers receive is top-down, with decisions about professional development removed from educators' classroom needs and concerns, lacking attention to systemic inequalities, and de-professionalizing teachers (Cochran-Smith & Lytle, 2009). In seeking to position students and parents as leaders who can teach schools about issues of equity, María Hernández, one of the Latine parents in the CARE Initiative, underscored that just as community knowledge is important, so too is the knowledge that teachers have of the system. María reframed the goal of "training teachers" in culturally relevant and anti-racist practices as a mutual learning opportunity, a way to be in dialogue with educators so that families could advocate for them to the school board and beyond. This stance of building coalitions across differences has been at the heart of our work.

One meaningful step toward fostering collaboration involved organizing a meeting between the families from the CARE Initiative and a school leader. On a Friday evening, parents and youth from the partnership gathered on Zoom with Raquel, a principal of a public school serving predominantly Latine families and who is herself a Latine immigrant. Olivia Vazquez Ponce, an organizer and community researcher, took the lead in organizing the sessions alongside a Latine college student who had been part of the CARE team for several years. Over the course of an hour and a half, members of the CARE Initiative had a chance to ask questions about the workings of one school where administrators and teachers were committed to anti-racist pedagogies, hearing details about the kinds of practices, dilemmas, and constraints that schools face. The families reciprocally shared the research they had been carrying out about school inequities, and their expectations for how schools can better serve children from Black, Brown, and immigrant communities. This included how parents could ensure their children's physical and emotional safety at school given the rise of anti-Asian violence and a resurgence of xenophobia and racism stoked by politicians. The dialogue was powerful and complicated, raising entrenched obstacles with no easy answers, moving across multiple languages, and crossing power differentials between educators and families. The youth and parents posed hard questions, drawing on their own research and their lived experiences as people of color navigating an unjust school system, and came together in solidarity across minoritized identities to engage in conversation with Raquel. The meeting was one step in the larger endeavor, spurred by community members, to work with educators to transform schools together and for the better.

These types of difficult and productive conversations do not just happen on their own. In this section, we explore how CBRE can create the conditions for navigating different perspectives as partners strive to build momentum and solidarity. Before bringing community researchers together with educational leaders, it is important to anticipate the challenges that could arise and address these proactively. Knowing that the perspectives of families of color are often devalued in educational spaces, we sought to be mindful of who the community researchers were initially entering into dialogue with and how the structure of the proposed event could center their knowledge and concerns. For us, this meant starting with leaders who were already addressing the intersections of race and justice in their schools and fostering a healing and critical space for families.

Prior to the event with the principal, the CARE Initiative members met to think together about the purpose of the meeting and the questions they wanted to ask. Drawing on their prior research the group generated a list of questions to guide the interaction (see Figure 5.4). These touched on the range of educational issues families were facing and harkened back to their demands for better schools that include rights to language access, anti-racist curricula, mental health supports, and rigorous academic opportunities. Families sought to learn about efforts schools were already making toward these goals as positive models that could inform future actions. They also wanted to know about the specific pressures that teachers, principals, and schools were facing so that they might advocate for them.

Olivia and her co-facilitator carried over the CARE Initiative's typical pedagogical practices to the dialogue, inviting the principal to a (virtual) community space that embodied the project norms of care and mutuality. The meeting began, as we generally do, with an icebreaker, allowing everyone to introduce themselves and get to know each other as people before moving on to the dialogue about educational equity. As the conversation got underway, Olivia invited family members and youth to pose questions to the principal. The ensuing discussion, though just a starting point in broader outreach and inquiry alongside teachers and leaders, allowed for the mutual exchange of ideas even as it highlighted the inherent challenges in working toward a vision of educational justice. Importantly, families and youth of color agentively shaped the conversation, asserting their epistemic rights as they sought to build consensus around ways to improve education. Below, we spotlight two moments to consider how to navigate such conversations with criticality and care.

Questions – Spanish:	English:
1. ¿Qué medidas toma para asegurarse de que los padres tengan acceso a la información de la escuela o a traductores?	1. What steps do you take to ensure that parents have access to information of the school or translators?
2. ¿Cómo nos aseguramos que el curriculum no sea eurocéntrico? ¿Cómo podemos asegurarnos de que los estudiantes aprendan sobre su historia?	2. How do we ensure that the curriculum is not Eurocentric? How can we ensure that students learn about their history?
3. ¿Cómo nos aseguramos que los niños reciban información de su idioma?	3. As we do ensure that children receive information in their native language.
4. ¿Desde la posición de liderazgo, cuáles son las áreas positivas? Qué se puede empujar para ayudar a familias? ¿Cómo se puede apoyar a los maestros?	4. From the leadership position, what are the positive areas? What can be done to support families? How can families support teachers?
5. ¿Qué tipo de poder tiene Ud. como directora?	5. What type of power does she as a principal have?
6. ¿Qué se puede hacer para que haya más maestros de color? ¿Cómo lo promueve en su escuela? En NYC hay mucha criminalización de los estudiantes, ¿cómo se puede combatir?	6. What can be done so that there are more teachers of color? How do you promote it in your school? In NYC there is a lot of criminalization of students, how can we fight back?
7. ¿Cómo asegura que a todos sus estudiantes les guste la escuela? Especialmente durante la pandemia	7. How do you make sure all your students like school? especially during the pandemic.
8. ¿Qué recursos hay para la salud mental de los estudiantes?	8. What resources are there for students' mental health?
9. ¿Qué tan apoyada se siente como directora, cuales son las barreras del distrito?	9. How supportive do you feel, what are the district's barriers that you faced?

Figure 5.4 Community-generated questions for dialogue with educational leader.

At one point, María Hernández posed the question of how parents can get access to school information, be further involved in classrooms, and support children with homework given the lack of translators and the hegemony of English. Principal Raquel explained how systemic challenges are manifested in schools, which historically are not designed to include families, and provided some illustrative examples of how she tries to think about communication differently in her school as she works within and against those constraints. María followed up:

María: Bueno, ¿puede añadir un poquitito más? Disculpa, gracias que me contestaste Raquel, pero bueno en realidad lo que quería tener un poquito más de idea—gracias por en general lo que dijiste, ayuda mucho—es que, como comentaste, cuando dan la tarea a los estudiantes que no saben pues le dejan el trabajo a los padres. Pero estamos como, ¿quién se echa la bolita? ¿Quién puede más que quién? A los estudiantes le decimos, "no entiendes," o "no pusiste atención," o "hazlo tú." Y los papás a veces decimos, "no tengo tiempo, no entiendo" y solamente estamos culpando. O "los maestros no explicaron, no hicieron su trabajo bien." Entonces como padres culpamos al estudiante y al maestro, como maestros culpan al estudiante y a los padres y los estudiantes a mi maestro o mis papás.

[Well, can I add a little bit more? Excuse me, thank you for what you answered Raquel, but in reality what I wanted was to have a little more of an idea—in general what you said helps a lot—is that as you commented, when students are given homework that they don't know, well the work is left to the parents. But we're like, who's passing the ball to whom? Who can do more than whom? To the students we say, "you don't understand," or "you didn't pay attention," or "do it yourself." And the parents, sometimes we say, "I don't have time, I don't understand," and we are only blaming. Or "the teachers didn't explain, they didn't do their job well." Then, as parents we blame the children and the teachers, and teachers blame the students and the parents, and the students, my teacher or my parents.]

Que estamos nada más culpándonos, pero no sabemos cómo tener la mejor comunicación ya que no todos los maestros y directores tienen esa flexibilidad de poder comunicarse con los padres o ser abiertos, como lo comentaste, de dar opciones cómo podemos comunicarnos. Entonces es ¿cómo mejorar esta comunicación para mejorar la educación? No es echarnos la culpa, quién puede o quién sabe, sino cómo mejorar y trabajar juntos. No sé si me entiende.

[We are only blaming each other, but we don't know how to have better communication, since not all the teachers and principals have that flexibility of being able to communicate with parents or being open as you commented, giving options of how we can communicate. Then, how to improve that communication to improve education? It's not about blaming each other, who can or who knows, but how to improve and work together. I don't know if you understand me.]

Raquel: Sí, sí, en – y escúseme por no responderlo cómo la pregunté. Lo que Usted me acaba de decir, y corríjame, es algo que nosotros como escuela hemos estado tratando también.

[Yes, yes, on – and excuse me for not responding according to what you asked me. I think that what you just said, and correct me, is something that we as a school have been trying too.]

In this interaction, María reframed the conversation in subtle ways that were both affirming of Raquel's contributions but shifted the focus to family partnerships with educators. Raquel had provided a thoughtful critique of how schools handle homework, noting that these practices typically do not account for multilingualism, caregivers' working conditions, and family situations that presented barriers to participation. Raquel's own background as a Dominican immigrant who entered the US school system in her youth and her subsequent efforts to support immigrant families as a teacher and principal informed her consideration of María's question. This response made clear Raquel's ideological stance about the sources of educational inequities, but it was not news to María or others in the group, who were living these challenges firsthand. In this moment, Raquel found herself engaging with a different audience of educational leaders and researchers: families themselves. Drawing on Elaine Castillo's (2022) concept of "the unexpected reader"—which she describes as "the arrival of someone who does not read them the way they expect—often demand—to be read; often someone who has been framed in their work and in their lives as an object, not a subject" (p. 63), María was, in this instance, an "unexpected researcher" in school conversations to engage families. She, and others in the CBRE project, were repositioning themselves as agentive subjects who can direct the conversation. As a principal committed to equity and justice, and as a Latina, Raquel was a fierce advocate for families, a commitment that shines through in her comments. These critical assertions about how the system works are sorely needed, yet in this context of CBRE, the readers of the educational status quo had already discerned these inequities and were advocating to start in a different place. As María notes, the work to be undertaken moves beyond abstract characterizations of the injustices of the system which pit different roles against each other through blaming and disputes about "who can or who knows." Rather, she argues that the purpose of partnerships centers on "how to improve and work together."

The conversation continues as Raquel apologizes for misunderstanding, and then goes on to provide concrete examples. She concludes her turn by asking: "Did I respond to your questions, Doña María?" María replies, "Thank you very much. You'll have to accompany us again because there are many more questions. But thank you." María and Raquel, both educational advocates for students of color, approached the topic of parent involvement from different vantage points. They used small cues to subvert the typical power dynamics among school administration and parents: María acknowledged the principal's contributions and perspectives but shifted the focus of the dialogue to coalitional solutions; Raquel followed the community researchers' lead by using terms signaling respect (e.g., the use of "Doña") and explicitly asking if her responses were accurate. María made space for others in the CBRE group to raise their questions but did not leave the matter "settled"—rather, she left the opening that Raquel join the group again for further discussions.

These trends continue with the input of other CARE members, such as Olivia Sr., an elder and activist in the Mexican community:

> Olivia: Maestra, yo le tengo una pregunta. Usted dijo algo muy cierto, estamos aprendiendo porque el aprendizaje es mutuo, ¿verdad? Pero ese es un problema que ya estamos viviendo real. La situación de usted es diferente porque usted es parte, usted creció en el sistema, usted vino también muy joven, entonces usted ha vivido el problema en carne propia. ¿Qué consejo nos puede dar usted a nosotros como padres para empujar a que este sistema con el que nosotros estamos navegando que no sabe los problemas reales que nosotros vivimos, cómo podemos empujar nosotros como padres al sistema para que nos apoye y trabajemos en conjunto? Porque sabemos la importancia de involucrarnos en la educación de nuestros hijos.
>
> Usted tiene experiencia de trabajar con la comunidad, usted ha sido parte de la comunidad, pero lamentablemente en el sistema en el que nosotros nos desenvolvemos, NO. ¿Cómo nosotros podemos empujar el sistema para que trabaje con nosotros y podamos superar todos estos problemas que estamos teniendo? Porque lo de la pandemia ya es un problema real que se está viviendo y estamos caminando con ello. ¿Pero cómo podemos empujar para cambiar todo esto?

[Maestra, I have a question. You said something very true; we are learning because learning is mutual, right? But it is a problem that we are really living. The situation with you (honorific) is different because you are part, you grew up in the system, you came here very young, you have lived the system in your own flesh. What advice can you give to us as parents to push so that this system that we are navigating, that doesn't know the real problems that we are living, how can we ourselves as parents push the system so that it supports us and we can work as a team? Because we know the importance of involving ourselves in the education of our children.

You have experience in working with the community, you have been part of the community, but unfortunately in the system that we are working within, NO. So, how can we push this system so that it works with us and we can overcome these problems that we are having? Because the pandemic is a real problem that we are living, and we are walking with it. But how can we push so that we can change all this?]

Raquel: Lo que yo siempre he—y gracias por su pregunta—siempre he pensado en cuáles son los mecanismos que existen para que las familias tengan una voz. Y lamentablemente muchas veces existen esos mecanismos, pero no están disponibles.

[What I always have, and thank you for your question, I have always thought about what are the mechanisms that exist so that families have a voice. And unfortunately, many times I think those mechanisms exist, but they are not available.]

Olivia Sr.'s comments make visible the shared identities between Raquel and the community researchers, but also highlights power dynamics among individuals from minoritized groups. As a language learner and immigrant to the US, Raquel had affinities with families from CARE. Yet, there are also differences in their racialized identities, migration histories, and institutional roles that make Raquel, as Olivia notes, an embodiment of the system, "having lived the system in (her) flesh," a conceptual insight perhaps reminiscent of Bourdieu's notion of habitus. It was another reminder, for all of us on the university-side of the partnership, that we too are embodiments and extensions of our own respective institutions, a fact that we should own and a form of privilege we should use for good, just like Raquel.

This interaction illustrates how we might begin to work through "insider" and "outsider" designations, make explicit issues of power, and cooperate in common cause. María Lugones' (2006) idea of complex communication is helpful in interpreting this exchange, which conceives coalition among minoritized communities as involving not a singular voice, but rather a polyvocality that in and of itself is "a disruption of the reduction attempted by the oppressor" (p. 84). Olivia's comment helps to expand the groups' understandings of Latine and immigrant communities by making explicit existing hierarchies as well as commonalities. She employs discourse of resistance prevalent in the immigrant rights organization with which she has been involved to communicate the importance of "pushing the system"—a system which has excluded families of color and mislabeled them as not invested in their children's education—and work "as a team." She channels the "coalitional potential of resistant anger" (Medina, 2020, p. 224) whereby emotions and historical legacies of fighting for change are part of the complex communication involved in navigating differences. As the examples illustrate, María and Olivia, like other parents and youth in the meeting, exhibit the agency to push past systemic critique or abstract academic explanations in order to ask: What can we all do in the here and now to improve education?

The interaction, like others in our work, did not resolve into an easy consensus where multiple perspectives were suppressed or domesticated, a critique that political philosophers such as Chantal Mouffe (2000) have of deliberative democracy. Importantly, however, neither did the conversations result in mere dissent and adversarial relations. The participants instead had a commitment to forwarding different perspectives while simultaneously being invested in the collective epistemic growth of the group and every individual's personal development and well-being. Medina (2013), in a critique of Mouffe, questions if the binary between consensus and dissensus is too stringent, and suggests we need to envision more possibilities for democratic engagement and responsiveness to one another. He argues for a radical solidarity which views others as "fellow member(s) of a community of experience and action mediated by a shared imagination that can give … common access to plural ways of imagining their past, present, and future" (p. 277). We believe that genuine solidarity has been forged in the CARE Initiative because the research is collectively directed through a commitment to care and reciprocity. Community researchers are not merely arguing for the rightness of their ideas, although they certainly make claims about the world derived from their research. They are also mining individual and group legacies, often ones that have been buried beneath histories of assimilation and colonization; enacting forms of educational community and sociality premised on interdependence, not individual competition; and inviting others to join their work of forging more just educational futures.

Questions for Reflection

1. What are your collaborative processes for consensus building around the direction of the research?
2. How are differing perspectives negotiated?
3. How might community members prepare to share their knowledge and challenge unjust systems?

References

Campano, G., Ghiso, M. P., & Thakurta, A. (2022). Community-based partnerships: Fostering epistemic rights through improvement focused research. In D. Peurach, J. L. Russell, L. Cohen-Vogel, & W. R. Penuel. (Eds.), *Foundational handbook on improvement-focused educational research* (pp. 189–210). Rowan & Littlefield.

Campano, G., Ngo, L., Low, D. E., & Jacobs, K. B. (2016). Young children demystifying and remaking the university through critical play. *Journal of Early Childhood Literacy, 16*(2), 199–227.

Castillo, E. (2022). *How to read now: Essays*. Viking Press.

Cochran-Smith, M., & Lytle, S. L. (2009). *Inquiry as stance: Practitioner research for the next generation*. Teachers College Press.

Cox, A. B. (2021). Powered down: The microfoundations of individual attempts to redistribute power. *American Journal of Sociology, 127*(2), 285–336.

Ghiso, M. P., Campano, G., Schwab, E., Asaah, G., & Rusoja, A. (2019). Mentoring in research-practice partnerships: Toward democratizing expertise. *AERA Open*, 5(4), 1–12.

Ghiso, M. P., Campano, G., Thakurta, A., & Vazquez Ponce, O. (2022). Community-based research with immigrant families: Sustaining an intellectual commons of care, resistance, and solidarity in an urban intensive context. *Urban Education* [online first], https://doi.org/10.1177/00420859221082676.

González, N., Moll, L. C., & Amanti, C. (Eds.). (2006). *Funds of knowledge: Theorizing practices in households, communities, and classrooms*. Routledge.

Ishimaru, A. M. (2019). *Just schools: Building equitable collaborations with families and communities*. Teachers College Press.

Lopez, G. (2009). The value of hard work: Lessons on parent involvement from an (Im)migrant household. *Harvard Educational Review, 71*(3), 416–438.

Lugones, M. (2006). On complex communication. *Hypatia, 21*(3), 75–85.

Medina, J. (2013). *The epistemology of resistance: Gender and racial oppression, epistemic injustice, and resistant imaginations*. Oxford University Press.

Medina, J. (2020). Complex communication and decolonial struggles: The forging of deep coalitions through emotional echoing and resistant imaginations. *Critical Philosophy of Race, 8*(1–2), 212–236.

Mouffe, C. (2000). For an agonistic public sphere. In J. Ockman (Ed.), *The pragmatist imagination* (pp. 66–73). Princeton University Press.

Yee, M., Mostafa, K., & Campano, G. (2016). Participatory research with parents: Mobilizing social capital to support children's education. In G. Campano, M. P. Ghiso, & B. J. Welch, *Partnering with immigrant communities: Action through literacy* (pp. 39–53). Teachers College Press.

6 How Does a CBRE Lens Inform Research Design?

Collaborative Data Collection and Analysis

The entrenched systemic challenges faced in the field of education *require* a bringing together of multiple perspectives and ways of knowing in the service of both critical discernment as well as the constructive project of imagining and building a better world. Yet academic training involves individuals spending years of their lives developing disciplinary methods in a specific area. How can those outside of academia be prepared for research?

As argued previously, we believe inquiry to be fundamentally the gathering of evidence to systematically investigate, interpret, and take action on an issue that impacts one's life. Research can be done in innumerable contexts and from a multiplicity of social locations. We embrace the universalism that all human beings, by virtue of being human, theoretically engage in inquiry. We have also suggested that those who are navigating oppressive systems are in a unique position to interpret the injustices that impact them and their communities. Inquiry is an act of survival, the air one breathes. For example, an undocumented youth or one from a mixed-status family will often have to be involved in hundreds of hours of research just to gain access to higher education. In the process, they may be able to discern patterns of inequity and power dynamics that may not be visible to individuals from dominant social backgrounds who may take access to college for granted because of their own citizenship status or relative familial affluence. Once in higher education, this same person may also employ, even repurpose, skills learned in academia to examine the issue of educational access from another angle, or even create a hybrid methodology that involves both institutional and community ways of knowing. Our point is to challenge the binary between academic and community knowledges and recognize that all people are potentially cosmopolitan intellectuals (Campano & Ghiso, 2011) who cross-fertilize ideas from the disparate contexts of their lives to critically interpret and engage the world.

What matters most in CBRE is that the methods of inquiry take seriously the intellectual agency, interests, and desires of everyone involved. One of the most creative and even joyful aspects of the CARE project has been to imagine and enact collaborative methods for data collection and interpretation, ones which may challenge calcified institutional norms where research perpetuates

DOI: 10.4324/9781003279686-6

academic discourse but does not serve the community in a tangible way. The community inquiries are not merely descriptive, characterizing the world as it is, but also speculative and even, inspired by Audre Lorde (Lorde, 1984), poetic: They may engender new ideas about teaching and learning as well as new ways of living and being in an intellectual community. Data collection thus has an ontological as well as epistemic dimension.

Expanding What Counts as Data

Designing research with communities entails rethinking processes and products for scholarly inquiry that typically hew toward academic audiences. In qualitative research, there have been efforts to expand forms of data collection through multimodality, photography, the arts, and culturally situated ways of knowing (e.g., Bhattacharya, 2013; Rose, 2012; Templeton, 2021), among other traditions. These approaches, in the spirit of epistemic pluralism, challenge "the hegemony of text-based knowledge in academic scholarship" (Literat et al., 2018, p. 565) and the hierarchies between "researchers" and those whose lives or experiences are "researched." In efforts to unsettle these dichotomies, it is important that reframing methods is *bidirectional*: not only that communities may acquire the power codes of "research" but that research designs be built on the practices of inquiry already existing in communities, including intergenerational forms of knowledge production and community legacies of societal interpretation. In designing CBRE, we must seek to understand what knowledge about the issue under study is always already present (but perhaps invisible to or not meant for academic audiences), what barriers to participation may be circumvented through expanding what counts as data, and how community cultural wealth (Yosso, 2005) may be central to data collection and analysis practices. For example, how communities of color generate knowledge through political organizing as well as everyday practices is central to methods such as pláticas (Flores Carmona et al., 2021), kitchen-table talks (Lyiscott et al., 2021), culture circles and community art (Rappaport, 2020; Sambolín Morales, 2022), or Double-Dutch methodologies (Green, 2011). Scholars have endured, and challenged, what Delgado Bernal and Villalpando (2002) refer to as "the apartheid of knowledge" to legitimate these types of cultural practices as forms of research within the academy.

In our work, the arts and multimodality have played a central role in research design. These approaches have expanded how we problem-pose (Freire, 1970), engage in data collection and analysis, and use findings to inform educational change. Embracing pluralism in methodological decisions requires epistemic humility on the part of university researchers, whose very institutional identities entail policing how to do research correctly. Rather than solely training community members in research methods beforehand, which implies the assimilation of youth, families, and communities into the discipline(s) of university-based research, we have found that understanding inquiry as socially and culturally situated practices enables a more bidirectional flow of knowledge. All members of the research team can engage with problems under study immediately through organic forms of inquiry already present in communities, and academic research concepts become threaded through the collective inquiry process rather than transmitted a priori. For example, we ourselves have learned so much from our partners about how to employ the arts to raise critical consciousness and agitate for change.

A research design centered on epistemic pluralism thus hybridizes multiple ways of knowing to create a collective interpretive horizon. We have had to be mindful of not privileging or defaulting to any singular methodological tool, but instead listening to community priorities about ways to study a problem and supporting openings for multiple avenues of investigation. When the CARE Initiative organizes teaching opportunities around specific methods, it has been based on group decisions and interests or because of dilemmas and questions that arise throughout the partnership. For example, Dr. Alexandra Thomas, who focuses on critical media-making, multimodal pedagogies, and curriculum design (Thomas, 2017), held a workshop for youth that taught printing within the context of how the arts have been used in activism and organizing. These crafting techniques were purposely selected because they had connections with the artistic legacies of the cultural and linguistic communities with whom we partner. Another year, we engaged in an inquiry into constructing surveys, which included discussing community members' prior—often negative—encounters with them and how they might be made more relational, culturally responsive, and attentive to the specific educational problems families were facing. The families' rationale for utilizing the respective methods involved thinking about the power of data for raising awareness about educational inequities. Families noted that the arts might have broad appeal for elevating the profile of pressing issues and making research accessible to members of the broader neighborhood community. The numbers derived from surveys might in turn carry weight when advocating for change at school board meetings, where an individual testimonial can be tied to larger patterns within the community. In these examples, the methodological expertise community partners were interested in was outside our own areas, necessitating outreach and expanding our networks. Other times doctoral students have led methods workshops for the group, including on topics such as writing fieldnotes or constructing interviews. Because inquiries into various research methods grow out of community interests, there are genuine opportunities for all to engage in joint learning.

Rethinking Data Collection and Ownership

CBRE necessitates rethinking "whose data" is being generated and recognizing data's situated nature. As many qualitative scholars have argued (e.g., Esposito & Evans-Winters, 2021; Liboiron, 2021), data does not exist "out there" for researchers to discover, but always involves power-laden decisions about, for example, what to look at or ignore, who is doing the looking and why, and how our frameworks inform what counts as data in any given context. We join scholars in using the term "data production" in addition to "data collection" (e.g., Kontovourki & Siegel, 2022) to underscore how data is a function of active meaning-making processes involving deliberate decisions and impacts. CBRE has an added collective valence to data production, whereby these decisions are themselves held up to scrutiny and must be actively negotiated with the community as part of the research. We produce data together through multi-perspectival inquiry, but no one individual "owns" the data—different individuals or groups of individuals have their own subjective research journeys and may draw from the data accordingly.

Academia, by contrast, privileges the proprietorship of data, casting research as belonging to individual researchers in ways that may obscure or erase the intellectual labor of others. The contributions of CBRE, however, cannot be arrived at by lone researchers, as the insights generated are an outgrowth of the creative synergies of collaborative inquiry and analysis. Decisions about how data is used must therefore be negotiated within the partnership and in the context of trusting relationships. Different research groups may develop varying approaches to how to make these decisions, such as by guidance from partnership norms (Campano et al., 2016a), memorandums arrived at in collective processes (e.g., McLaughlin & London, 2013), or thinking through specific decisions as opportunities arise.

CBRE may invariably require the suspension of habitual ways of doing research, spurred by pressures of time and productivity, to reflect on everyone's right to research and to the larger project goals. For example, a community center may feel an urgency to submit quantifiable "deliverables" such as an impact report, to procure or renew grant funding that would keep the lights on or provide supplies for an afterschool enrichment program. University-based researchers may feel the pressure to prioritize publications in the prestigious scholarly venues of their fields. It is not easy to navigate these demands in ethical ways that are respectful of communities and do not put undue burden on their time and energy. CBRE requires all of us to take a step back, especially when things seem urgent. Open and transparent discussions about data—where it is housed, who has access to it, and what we want to do with it individually and collectively—are part of the recursive processes we discussed in Chapter 5. The virtues of critical empathy, solidarity, and epistemic pluralism help us navigate questions about data and research design and ensure that individuals do not become alienated from their intellectual and scholarly labor.

Multi-Perspectival Inquiry and Analysis

Different disciplinary approaches in education have critiqued positivist images of the dispassionate researcher who sheds bias and is able to procure unmediated access to the phenomenon being studied. As we discussed earlier in this chapter, researchers are always part of a study—drawing on their own identities, frameworks, and ways of knowing across all aspects of research. The foundation of CBRE as shared research that centers the perspectives of communities directly impacted by educational inequities necessitates rethinking data analysis as a collective and multi-perspectival process.

It is worth pausing here to reflect on the difference between neutrality and objectivity. People are always analyzing from a particular social location and ideological lens. As opposed to a "bias" to be eliminated or minimized, these locations can be affordances for knowledge production, because people's interpretive frameworks—in particular, their epistemic privilege (Campano, 2007; Moya, 2002) toward understanding social inequities—can offer a counter, and more objective explanation to dominant understandings of a problem. Just because someone's perspective is not neutral does not imply that their analysis is relativistic or unable to approximate truth. As Alcoff (2007) notes, one's identity does not "yield knowledge in and of itself, but that it contains resources from which new knowledges can be developed with critical and theoretical reflection" (p. 46). In CBRE, this critical and theoretical reflection occurs through the collective production and analysis of data in communities of inquiry. We argue that a robust diversity of situated perspectives and identities affords an opportunity to get a fuller, more accurate and nuanced understanding of the phenomenon being studied.

To illustrate, we return to the nascent research being conducted by CARE youth who are documenting community resistance to the proposed stadium that threatens Philadelphia's Chinatown. Residents—youth, families, store owners, and community leaders—are offering a counter-narrative to the pitch provided by the city's sports team, which is funding studies to argue that the stadium is going to benefit the community by creating jobs and revitalizing the city center. Residents and long-time activists bring other experiences to their own interpretive horizons, which inform their analysis of the situation. Some have researched Chinatowns across the nation which have been disappeared as the result of similar "revitalization initiatives." Others have acquired hard-earned knowledge about the propaganda tactics of builders who have dispossessed and displaced Black and Brown residents in city neighborhoods. And several elders have successfully fought to defend Chinatown in the past and learned from these organizing efforts. These community researchers are critically reading "up the ladder of privilege" (Mohanty, 2003, p. 511) to contest the arguments and evidence of dominant social groups who may have "a pattern of belief-forming practices" that results in the "systematic ignorance" (Alcoff, 2007, p. 48) of inequality. Communities of inquiry can pool from a multiplicity of experiences to defend themselves from intersectional forms of oppression, harnessing the collective knowledge of the group.

We want to be cautious that our arguments for multi-perspectival inquiry do not romanticize the process or homogenize perspectives along identity categories. Members of a community of inquiry, including ones composed predominantly of minoritized researchers, will invariably bring nuanced and complex viewpoints to bear on an issue. We have found that exploring the dissonances that arise throughout the research process with empathy and care can lead to more robust research findings. In one inquiry cycle from the CARE Initiative, for example, families were ethnographically documenting the material conditions of schools, taking photos of what spaces of learning looked like across the city, from the bathrooms to the cafeteria lunches to the hallways. A photograph from the neighborhood high school, depicting metal detectors flanking its entrance, sparked debate. In discussing this image, Michael, one of the Indonesian youth, recalled the terror of experiencing active shooter drills at his school and the emotional and physical toll of recent high-profile school shootings across the nation. He expressed his concern about the possibility of an armed gunman gaining entrance to his school and argued for the need for increased security measures. María, a Latina mother with children in the public school system, talked about the over-policing of schools attended by students of color and drew on her knowledge as an immigrant activist to underscore the discrepant ways school security is enacted across contexts to criminalize Black and Latine students. Both perspectives are grounded in very rational concerns and the goal that children have safe places to learn. In discussing further, the group identified how, while ostensibly fine on their own, the individual research interpretations were leading to contesting conclusions and ideas for action—with one perspective arguing for the need for greater security and the other calling to interrogate public education's complicity with the carceral state, as schools increasingly resemble and function as prisons. Within this intersectional context, the conflict between María's and Michael's perspectives and experiences created an opening for further dialogue.

Reflecting on the collective work of community-based research, María commented, "Aprendí a escuchar y a entender un poco más opiniones y perspectivas diferentes de cada persona. Compartir, bromear, respetar, aprender uno de otro" ["I learned to listen and understand a bit more the different opinions and perspectives of each person. To share, joke, respect, learn from one another"]. María underscored the value of listening to youth and the atmosphere of care that makes collaboration across differences possible. Michael and other members of the research team gained important perspectives from María's caring interactions, which eventually helped them name the disparate experiences Asian-American and Latine youth might have with law enforcement. They also began to speculate about a coalitional vision of safety, one that gets at the root causes of why students should fear any violence at all in their schools, whether state sanctioned or from a lone perpetrator. Together, as a community of inquiry and with an ethics of care, individuals were able to grapple with the valences of an issue and deepen their respective understandings.

Research Design Examples

In this section, we delve into two related inquiries from our CBRE partnership that utilized photography to understand families' experiences with the public education system and the link between education and other social justice issues impacting communities of color in the city. We marquee these examples to illustrate how a CBRE approach might inform research design. We believe the inquiries also speak to the iterative nature of research within the context of long-term partnerships: Learnings from the first project, begun in 2015, would go on to inform our most current endeavor, which began in 2022.

Inquiring into Schooling

Since its inception, families' relationship to schooling has been a topical thread running through the CARE partnership, but in 2015 it became an explicit focus of inquiry. We were inspired by research from Dr. Tarajean Yazzie-Mintz and members of the Wakanyeja "Sacred Little Ones" initiative (American Indian College Fund, n.d.) to improve early childhood education within Native communities. Their work was methodologically grounded in a strength-based perspective: the families' own values and understandings of early childhood flourishing. We learned from the Sacred Little Ones project how the arts—specifically photography—helped concretize indigenous communities' visions for education as rooted in their own languages, histories, and cultural identities and spurred further inquiry. Members of the Sacred Little Ones project noted that themes which surfaced from the images would eventually help inform program development, teacher learning initiatives, and other locally situated efforts at educational change (e.g., Lansing, 2022). At an AERA conference symposium session based on this work (Akee & Yazzie-Mintz, 2015), attendees interacted with large-sized, vibrant photographs on easels representing Native families' visions of early childhood education, a beautiful exhibition and powerful reminder that the photos were both a tool for inquiry and a way to make public the fruits of research. These were lessons we sought to share and potentially adapt as part of the CARE Initiative. Dr. Yazzie-Mintz generously visited our research collective to be a thought partner as we took up related questions in ways that were responsive to our own context and local concerns.

We invited families to use photography to document community resources to support children's education as well as the barriers they have experienced. Looking back on the goals families had shared at vision-setting sessions and informed by one-on-one meetings with different members of the group, we structured a series of inquiry conversations around three related questions: What are the ways in which your family already supports your children's education? What are the barriers and challenges you face? And what hopes do you have for changes in the educational system? For each round of investigation, individuals shared their photographs, alongside related stories, anecdotes, experiences, and writings that were sparked by them. These artifacts became the impetus for exploring systemic issues like school funding, the narrowing of curricula, and police presence in schools. The end goal, after these cycles of photographic inquiry, would be to gain a better understanding of how schools could learn from communities, specifically communities of color, and how those of us who are part of the partnership could work together to support children's education.

As we sat in a circle and opened the floor for conversation, different members of the group took turns describing photographs they had brought. Daria unlocked her phone and showed a picture of her grandson's first day at college. The extended family—grandmother, mother, and younger siblings—had gone to drop him off and had spent the day helping to set up his dorm room and acclimate to campus. The picture underscored the intergenerational nature of family educational involvement while also helping to familiarize the college-going process for younger generations. It kindled a conversation about the importance of discussing college with youth, even young children, a thread that would eventually materialize into an Inquiry into College (Campano et al., 2016b; Ghiso et al., 2022). A Latine high school student noted the challenges she was encountering in "not knowing what to study" at college, and that she would welcome help in how to prepare for those choices. Parents and youth also voiced financial concerns regarding the cost of college and how to seek avenues for funding, including the fact that financial aid often required disclosure of immigration status, which could put families at risk.

Next, an elder in the Indonesian community showed a picture of children, including her two daughters, in traditional Indonesian dress at one of the parish masses. She described how teaching her children their culture was an important part of their education. The intersection of language and culture was a topic that María had taken up as well, and she went on to share her images. María had created a poster that included many pictures of her family as well as an essay about some of her thoughts.

María asserted that as parents, she and her husband were "ayudando a nuestros hijos que tengan un mejor futuro en su educación" ["helping their children have a better future in their education"]. The first tenet she named in their support was, "estamos enseñando que siempre deben respetar a las personas así como los lugares a donde se encuentran" ["we are teaching them that they must always respect people as well as the places they find themselves"]. She commented that she wrote her text in Spanish because in her home that is the language they speak, even though everywhere else people demanded English only, noting that she often hears exhortations of "you live in America, you have to talk English." María described how she helped prepare their children for the future by speaking Spanish with them and encouraging community involvement. These activities included sports, literature discussion groups, the arts, and gatherings specifically geared to the Latine community as well ones where her children would mingle with youth from diverse backgrounds. María commented, "if children come together, they will learn from each other and there will be less racism."

The ensuing conversation took up the topic of linguistic hierarchy. María recounted how her daughter went to school and was having trouble communicating in English. One time she asked, "why don't you speak English with me?" María responded that she would have plenty of time in school to learn English. At home, she would learn Spanish so that she was guaranteed to know two languages. A high school student noted that these priorities reflected the values of her own family and her mother's refrain that "it is important to maintain your culture"—wisdom she embraced by taking Catechism formation classes in Spanish and learning to read and write in Spanish outside school contexts.

A mother and son from the Indonesian community presented next, continuing to elaborate on the intersections of migration, language, and cultural identity. The mother showed a picture of the two of them reading the Bible in Indonesian together. She told us that although she has been in the U.S. for some time, it was only in the past two years that her son had been able to join her. Most of his childhood, she got to know him over FaceTime while he was being cared for by her parents. The mother noted her goals to support their Indonesian language and cultural identity in the home, but that he is still learning English to be successful in the U.S. One way she was maintaining their Indonesian connection is by reading the Bible in Indonesian every night, the only book she had in their native language, which was helping her get to know her son and deepen their relationship as they prayed, talked, and cared for each other. The mother persevered in devoting time to these literacy activities at home—what she called "a very special time"—despite working long hours. During the discussion, her son shared the challenge he was facing in adapting to a new context and language, a sentiment to which many others in the group could relate.

In a subsequent inquiry session, members of the research collective continued these topical leitmotifs. María's son showed the group an image of his math homework and explained the challenges it presented for families who spoke a language other than English. The assignment was a Home Link exploring volume, to be completed at home, and read:

> Collect some containers that are different shapes and sizes, such as cottage cheese cartons, plastic bottles, and juice containers. Use the containers to pour water back and forth. Try to find out which container holds the most, which holds the least, and which containers hold about the same amount.

In a boxed note on the top of the page, families are advised that "bath time provides an excellent opportunity to experiment and play with these containers."

María and her son recounted how they stayed up until midnight going word by word through the dictionary, trying to discern the meaning of the assignment and complete it within the given time frame. María added their frustration that despite these efforts, teachers never gave feedback on the homework, even after she approached them about it, because it was too much work. This example, one of many, crystalized for the group that many school exercises have a generic monolingual, Anglo, middle-class family in mind, rather than attending to the particularities of community experiences. On the surface, this homework artifact showcases an exploratory activity designed to give students the opportunity to play with mathematical concepts, like volume, that they might encounter in daily life. Yet these "home links" (as the home-work handout refers to them) presuppose certain cultural and class-based norms as well as that the language and content of the exercise are transparent. These presumptions render parents' efforts to mediate schooling requirements invisible and deficitizes them for not being adequately "engaged" with their children's education.

The group brought a range of other issues to the table as well, including the following: bullying, the middle school and high school admissions processes, college debt, and racism in the curriculum. Throughout the inquiry, we all learned about educational inequities that impact particular groups, such as undocumented and mixed-status families. This required individuals to decenter their own respective experiences while gaining thick descriptions of the agency of families in supporting and advocating for educational access, despite the barriers they face. One of the CARE community elders, Daria, has modeled for the whole group the kind of critical empathy required for understanding the complexities of shared social spaces, such as the parish and schools, and forging cross-racial solidarity. As the founder of the parish's Concerned Black Catholics group, a neighborhood block captain, and long-time resident of the area, Daria developed the skill of listening to and affirming the experiences of newer immigrant families while simultaneously situating them within local histories of segregation, anti-Black racism, and coalitional community movements from decades earlier. Her advocacy and persistence, coupled with her genuine love and support for others in the group, was for-mative in making race central to the conversation about educational access. Daria's insights were echoed by others who had been involved in grassroots organizing linking race and immigration, thus avoiding the bifurcation of issues along narrow identitarian boundaries, countering the race-evasiveness of many immigrant families, and paving the way for more systemic analyses that reverberated well into future inquiries.

Our analysis sessions were structured with the same ethos and principles as our other meetings, with attention to the pedagogies of CBRE discussed in Chapter 5. In this way, there was not a tangible difference in the "data pro-duction" and "data analysis" sessions, between the *conducting the inquiry* and *reflecting on the inquiry process*, because participants moved across these roles as co-researchers rather than as objects of study. We created

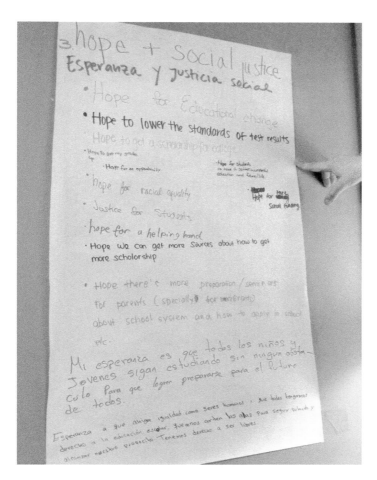

Figure 6.1 CARE members charting their interpretation of goals for educational justice.

interactive opportunities for people to revisit the ideas and artifacts related to the inquiry questions, to look for patterns across the experiences while still accounting for discrepancies, and to think about the implications of the findings. The sessions sought to provide ample and expansive openings for all members to participate, including through multiple languages and interactive conversations (e.g., Figure 6.1)—presuming everyone's interpretive capacities rather than a need to be "trained" in academic analysis.

We also created posters of their findings (see Figure 6.2, 6.3, and 6.4) which were placed around the community center, distributed to various interested audiences, and shared publicly at community forums as well as in presentations to educators.

Figure 6.2 Analysis of community strengths.

The members of the CARE Initiative then distilled a list of "demands" for educational equity which were logical outgrowths of their analysis and findings (Campano et al., 2016a). These included smaller class sizes, attention to language access such as through community liaisons and translation services, academic and internship opportunities for all students, that schools use ITIN numbers instead of social security numbers for parent involvement and volunteering, that teachers receive training in addressing racism and honoring diversity, that academic support be offered after school so that children are not pulled out from mainstream classes, and "that schools and teachers see the strengths and intelligence in all of our children and work with families to build on our children's strengths." The language of "demands" is one that

Figure 6.3 Analysis of systemic obstacles.

carried over from families' involvement in grassroots political organizing and speaks to how community knowledge has been transforming the nature of research. As opposed to "findings," which signal an end to the inquiry process and connote a kind of stasis, "demands" are forward-looking and action oriented. This shift frames research as a part of the continued and evolving struggle for educational equity.

Inquiring into Social Movements

The CARE Initiative demands reflect the epistemic advantage of collaborative and multi-perspectival approaches to data production and analysis for addressing intersectional forms of oppression. To truly support educational justice, the CARE members argued, we need to shed light and take action on all factors impacting students, including economic precarity, the policing of

Figure 6.4 Analysis of future actions.

communities of color, and forced displacement due to gentrification and/or the shuttering of neighborhood schools (e.g., Campano et al., 2013). Several youth would thus become inspired to inquire into and participate in city-wide campaigns to address these issues.

Our most recent inquiry, currently underway, seeks to leverage CBRE to support Chinatown residents in their fight to protect their neighborhood from plans by billionaire developers to build a sports stadium one block away, as discussed in previous chapters. A number of youth involved in CARE grew up in Chinatown or attended one of its schools, started by community activists, which has as part of its mission a focus on equity and justice for immigrant students. Beginning with the context of Chinatown specifically, the inquiry evolved to investigate the impact of "development projects" on communities and, by implication, families' educational opportunities. The youth proposed a photovoice and interview research project that would invite residents of Chinatown, and other endangered city neighborhoods, to share their own stories, just as they had done themselves. This prompted self-reflexive discussions on the ethics of research methods.

In the youth sessions to co-design this inquiry, we have paid special attention to inquiring into the power dynamics and cultural dimensions of interviewing. How, for example, can we think about non-extractivist and anti-colonial approaches to interviewing? We have tried to be mindful of not trans-mitting to youth a step-by-step protocol for composing and asking interview questions, as if these processes could be detached from the group's ethical and professional norms. We decided to invite alumni scholars from the CARE Initiative to lead an interviewing workshop for the youth (see Figure 6.5). The three scholars continue to research together, with the latest iteration of their work centered on interviews, so they had some fresh thinking on the method (Rusoja et al., 2023). Because they all had been both part of the CARE team and were organizers, they were also in a unique position to discuss interviewing neighborhood activists who were in the midst of a campaign. They discussed how culture, language, and race intersect with the interview process, and our ethical commitments to the stories gifted by others, espe-cially during such politically contentious times. Alongside CARE doctoral students Claire and Jackie, the youth then interviewed community elders and, also, one another. Being both an interviewer and an interviewee reinforces that knowledge construction is always bidirectional and the goal is to create a community of shared meaning. Through the already-established trusting relationships and practices of intergenerational mentorship, youth received feedback and guidance on how to embody CBRE principles through their specific practices of data collection.

Youth spent time in subsequent sessions analyzing interviews together. They looked over transcripts (Figure 6.6) and marked recurrent themes, new

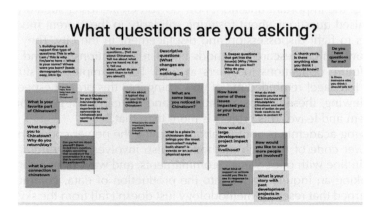

Figure 6.5 Sample questions from the community interviewing workshop.

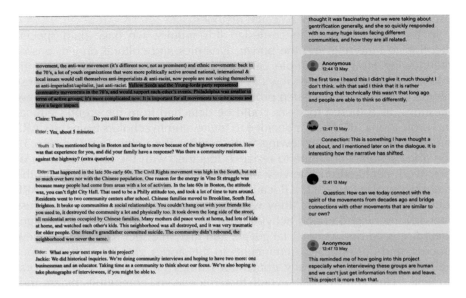

Figure 6.6 Collectively analyzed interview transcript.

questions, connections with previous data, and poignant lines that stood out (e.g., "Chinatown goes beyond geographical boundaries").

The analysis led to discussions about one's obligation to others, past and present. For instance, Lukas wondered, "How can we connect with the spirit of the movements from decades ago and bridge connections with other movements that are similar to our own?" Another high school-aged researcher noted that the interviewee, "emphasizes the criticality of fostering communal connections, unity, and collaboration—especially in activism. It certainly reminds me of the important question: how do you create/foster such unity?" The youth raised questions about fostering solidarity in the current moment across efforts to fight dispossession and displacement in the city. They also discussed how ethical research methods entail real relationships and may necessitate future obligations to others as well. For example, one student noted, "This [passage] reminded me of how going into this project especially when interviewing, these groups are human, and we can't just get information from them and leave. This project is more than that."

Demystifying academia is not just about learning the power codes, in this case the power code of research methods. It also involves transforming the codes to be in line with one's values, commitments, and ways of being in the world. By taking an inquiry stance into the production of data, community members learned that research methodology just doesn't fall from the sky and is not merely the purview of the hyper-schooled. There are organic practices of inquiring into the world that grow out of one's everyday lived experiences. Disciplinary methods are also useful tools as well. They too can be learned, critically unpacked, and creatively repurposed to meet community research goals. In CBRE the goals are not just about accurately discerning underlying patterns of inequity, but also about breaking these patterns in order to create more just social arrangements, in school and beyond.

Questions for Reflection

1. How are research questions collaboratively generated?
2. What research methods will guide your inquiries? How do these methods intersect with the philosophical groundings of CBRE?
3. How might the data be collaboratively analyzed? How will the data and findings become part of a shared intellectual commons?

References

Akee, R., & Yazzie-Mintz, T. (2015). *Shifting Native early childhood education: Toward justice and inclusive family engagement at the earliest levels of education.* American Educational Research Conference, Chicago, IL.

Alcoff, L. M. (2007). Epistemologies of ignorance: Three types. In S. Sullivan & N. Tuana (Eds.), *Race and epistemologies of ignorance* (pp. 39–57). SUNY Press.

Bhattacharya, K. (2013). Voices, silences, and telling secrets: The role of qualitative methods in arts-based research. *International Review of Qualitative Research*, 6(4), 604–627.

Campano, G. (2007). *Immigrant students and literacy: Reading, writing, and remembering.* Teachers College Press.

Campano, G., & Ghiso, M. P. (2011). Immigrant students as cosmopolitan intellectuals. In S. Wolf, K. Coates, P. Enciso, & C. Jenkins (Eds.), *Handbook of research on children's and young adult literature* (pp. 164–176). Routledge.

Campano, G., Ghiso, M.P., Yee, M., & Pantoja, A. (2013). Community research and coalitional literacy practices for educational justice. *Language Arts*, 90(5), 314–326.

Campano, G., Ghiso, M. P., & Welch, B. (2016a). *Partnering with immigrant communities: Action through literacy.* Teachers College Press.

Campano, G., Ngo, L., Low, D. E., & Jacobs, K. B. (2016b). Young children demystifying and remaking the university through critical play. *Journal of Early Childhood Literacy*, 16(2), 199–227.

Delgado Bernal, D. D., & Villalpando, O. (2002). An apartheid of knowledge in academia: The struggle over the "legitimate" knowledge of faculty of color. *Equity & Excellence in Education*, 35(2), 169–180.

Esposito, J., & Evans-Winters, V. (2021). *Introduction to intersectional qualitative research.* Sage.

Flores Carmona, J., Hamzeh, M., Delgado Bernal, D., & Hassan Zareer, I. (2021). Theorizing knowledge with pláticas: Moving toward transformative qualitative inquiries. *Qualitative Inquiry*, 27(10), 1213–1220.

Freire, P. (1970). *Pedagogy of the oppressed.* Continuum.

Ghiso, M. P., Campano, G., Thakurta, A., & Vazquez Ponce, O. (2022). Community-based research with immigrant families: Sustaining an intellectual commons of care, resistance, and solidarity in an urban intensive context. *Urban Education* [online first]. https://doi.org/10.1177/00420859221082676

Green, K. (2011). Doing Double Dutch methodology: Playing with the practice of participant observer. In D. Paris & M. T. Winn (Eds.), *Humanizing research: Decolonizing qualitative inquiry with youth and communities* (pp. 147–160). Sage.

Kontovourki, S., & Siegel, M. (2022). "B is for bunny": Contested sign-making and the possibilities for performing school literacy differently. *Read Research Quarterly*, 57(1), 111–129.

Lansing, D. R. (2022). Engaging Native families in co-creating meaningful educational opportunities as a community. In J. Garcia, V. Shirlie, & H. A. Kulago (Eds.), *Indigenizing education: Transformative research, theories, and praxis* (pp. 213–229). Information Age Publishing.

Liboiron, M. (2021). *Pollution is colonialism*. Duke University Press.

Literat, I., Conover, A., Herbert-Wasson, E., Page, K. K., Riina-Ferrie, J., Stephens, R., Thanapornsangsuth, S., & Vasudevan, L. (2018) Toward multimodal inquiry: Opportunities, challenges and implications of multimodality for research and scholarship. *Higher Education Research & Development, 37*(3), 565–578.

Lorde, A. (1984). *Sister outsider: Essays and speeches*. Crossing Press.

Lyiscott, J., Green, K., Ohito, E., & Coles, J. (2021). Call us by our names: A kitchen-table dialogue on doin' it for the culture. *Equity & Excellence in Education, 54*(1), 1–18.

McLaughlin, M. & London, R. A. (Eds.). (2013). *From data to action: A community approach to improving youth outcomes*. Harvard Education Press.

Mohanty, C. T. (2003). "Under Western eyes" revisited: Feminist solidarity through anticapitalist struggles. *Signs: Journal of Women in Culture and Society, 28*(2), 499–535.

Moya, P. (2002). *Learning from experience: Minority identities, multicultural struggles*. University of California Press.

Rappaport, J. (2020). *Cowards don't make history: Orlando Fals Borda and the origins of participatory action research*. Duke University Press.

Rose, G. (2012). *Visual methodologies: An introduction to researching with visual methods*. Sage.

Rusoja, A., Portillo, Y., & Vazquez Ponce, O. (2023). "Mi lucha es tu lucha; tu lucha es mi lucha": Latinx immigrant youth organizers facilitating a new common sense through coalitional multimodal literacies. *International Journal of Qualitative Studies in Education, 36*(3), 487–507.

Sambolín Morales, A. (2022). Motherwork post-displacement: Love, trust, and kinship through Freirean culture circles. *The Educational Forum, 86*(4), 368–381.

Templeton, T. (2021). Whose story is it? Thinking through early childhood with young children's photographs. *Occasional Paper Series, 2021*(45). https://doi.org/10.58295/2375-3668.1391

Thomas, D. A. (2017). *Navigating transnational borderlands through critical media-making* (Publication No. 10285512) [Doctoral Dissertation, Teachers College, Columbia University]. ProQuest Dissertations Publishing.

Yosso, T. J. (2005). Whose culture has capital? A critical race theory discussion of community cultural wealth. *Race, Ethnicity, and Education, 8*(1), 69–91.

7 What Does It Mean to Go Public with Research in CBRE?

Scholarship as Intellectual Activism

Early on in the CARE Initiative, we shared insights from the partnership at an academic conference of educational researchers and teachers. During the question-and-answer period, an attendee asked why community members were not co-presenters alongside us, and if we had plans to write collaboratively with our partners. The answer is more complicated than might initially appear. The reflex response is a resounding "yes," but we have deliberated over the contradictions and potential impositions of this ostensibly inclusive undertaking. Whose plans and visions for research are served when the dissemination of research happens within a primarily academic sphere? How can research reach a wide array of audiences, from families and teachers to researchers and legislators? What kind of (and whose) labor is involved in sharing research? How do partners envision the impact of the work and what are generative ways to reach that impact? Why, how, and where to go public with research findings in CBRE remain for us ongoing questions. They are fundamental to understanding and advancing a robust vision of participatory justice for communities and families who have historically been excluded from decisions of policy and practice in education.

In the CARE Initiative, going public has extended across academic and community contexts. One imperative for CBRE is to create opportunities for collaborative writing and presentations in scholarly spaces—thus helping make the contributions of students, families, educators, and community leaders more visible to university-based researchers, fostering direct dialogue among multiple stakeholders in projects for educational equity, and amplifying collaborative research paradigms. At the same time, academia is not necessarily the preferred context for sharing research findings, and we must follow community partners' lead about local levers of change. CBRE aims to reach multiple audiences, a goal that entails thinking expansively about the modes and contexts for communicating its findings. In this chapter, we focus on several examples of how the CARE Initiative has gone public with its research over the years, energized by the talents of different members of the partnership. We discuss our efforts to make the sharing of research a positive

DOI: 10.4324/9781003279686-7

experience for community members, doing our best to ensure that their intellectual labor is spotlighted and productively engaged.

Collaborative Conference Presentations

A primary venue for sharing the research of the CARE Initiative has indeed been scholarly conferences, including the Annual Meeting of the American Educational Association, The National Council of Teachers of English Conference, and the University of Pennsylvania's Ethnography and Education Conference. These presentations have been valuable to the group because they have helped to demystify academia. By the time many of the youth have entered college, for example, they have presented their original research at numerous scholarly convenings under the guidance of university doctoral students and faculty. Throughout these various stagings of their work, we have been intentional about co-creating academic experiences that do not reproduce harm. More than just reporting on findings, the conference events become an opportunity for further inquiry into how to engage a range of audiences, including researchers, teachers, and school leaders. This requires substantial preparation beyond designing posters or PowerPoint slides (Thakurta et al., 2021) on the elements of their research (e.g., conceptual framework, research question, methods, etc.).

One way the CARE Initiative has prepared presenters is through role playing and drama-based inquiry. Doctoral students and Youth Research Fellows, who had previous experience in the genre of the scholarly conference, have designed simulations of the types of questions and interactions community researchers might expect. This gives them practice in making arguments and claims, derived from their data, in real-time, something they would have to do in the question-and-answer period of a presentation or in small group discussions during a roundtable, poster session, or an alternative format such as a symposium. For example, before one conference where the older youth (middle and high schoolers) were presenting, the group simulated a roundtable discussion with an audience of family members and elders, who provided thoughtful feedback, and the youth kept notes on the types of questions and topics which surfaced. At the end of the round table rehearsal, the whole group responded to one of the following prompts: 1) Students: What did you learn today from parents? and 2) Parents: What did you learn today from students? The rehearsal helped prepare youth for the conference, but it also became an intergenerational dialogue. This is important in the CARE Initiative, because many of the parents and elders in the group went to school in countries outside the United States. The parents could learn about what the youth were experiencing in their schools and the youth, in turn, could better understand and contextualize their parents' own perspectives on education and aspirations for them.

The simulations also helped bolster the presenters' confidence. During a practice session, one of the youth presenters began to tear up a bit as his nerves got to him. Two peers in his group encouraged him by giving him space to collect himself, putting a hand on his shoulder, and guiding him to read the notecards he had prepared. With support, the youth gained self-assurance about his ideas and ability to communicate them. At the actual conference, he was the star, explaining cogently to a large audience of educators how youth of color are disadvantaged when it comes to college access and unpacking the racialized tracking mechanisms in his school district. It was a poignant moment for the whole group, given his earlier apprehension, and we were all so proud of him.

Preparation also involves discussing the types of power dynamics which the youth may encounter at an academic conference. For example, there may be educators who are not open to hearing youth perspectives. Families may also be made to feel as if they do not belong, and we have had several unfortunate incidences where individuals have been initially denied entry into a conference event because of assumptions that they are not registered, despite time-consuming efforts to ensure that would not happen. We try to be mindful about attending conferences which we believe will be a receptive space for dialogue. When deciding on scholarly outlets for our work, we have looked to organizations (or divisions and special interest groups within organizations) that have a proven track record of equity, of valuing the knowledge of communities of color, and of welcoming families and youth.

We have also worked within the existing conference structure to choose formats that align with the purposes the group deems most appropriate for any given research focus. This might include poster presentations or alternative format sessions that invite discussion with researchers from other participatory and community-based research initiatives, or ones that have extended time to allow everyone a chance to contribute. Being aware of the unpredictability of conference attendance, we try to promote our sessions to colleagues who have similar interests. Community partners make sacrifices to attend, and we owe it to them to do everything in our power to make it a meaningful event. Conference presentations have also reaped benefits beyond the actual research dissemination. They are bonding experiences that strengthen trust. If the conference is in another city or university, we always plan meals and other local activities, such as visits to aquariums, museums, local parks, or tours of the area. Even the bus rides together have sparked many moments of joyful connection and irreverence.

Conference presenting has been a significant vehicle for CARE Initiative members to exercise their epistemic rights and advance participatory justice for their communities in scholarly spaces that are generally exclusive. Because conferences are sites of inquiry, attending them is not about assimilating into academia, but rather about deepening the group's critical understandings of higher education and sometimes even speaking back to educational research, policy, and practice. Since the onset of Covid, digital formats have enabled members of the CARE partnership to present with fewer expenses and logistical hurdles. Though virtual formats cannot approximate the collective sense of adventure involved in a conference journey or foster the bonding that comes with such in-person assembly, we have nonetheless had many meaningful interactions online. For example, several community researchers presented their research on a Zoom call to Gerald's doctoral seminar for educational leaders, including superintendents, principals, and teachers, several of whom worked in the youth's own school district. Those leaders expressed that it was one of the most powerful and edifying moments in their studies. One of them commented:

> Watching the youth participants of the CARE Initiative impacted me on three different levels. As a Filipinx, child of Asian-Immigrants, it was healing for me to see youth who look like me advocate for themselves and make their voices audible to local issues and conversations. I felt so hopeful for the future and inspired by their research, activism, and passion. As an educator, it was a reminder that including youth and families' voices is necessary. It takes a village to raise, educate, and build the next leaders of our future. Finally, as an education leader, it was transformative to witness how typical definitions of leadership were turned on their heads. The youth and community members exemplified how leadership means working with each other—leadership for the community, by the community, and with the community. The synergies of all their knowledge, experience, and leadership are the catalyst for a better future.

Organizing moments when community researchers can spotlight their work to individuals with power in schools brings needed attention to educational issues, spurring leaders to consider how these obstacles show up in their own contexts. Such presentations also highlight youth's and families' deep investment in advocating for change, potentially "catalyzing" different relationships among educational leaders and the broader communities which schools serve.

There are also times when we discuss the project without the presence of community members. When we go to a conference that they are unable to attend, we strive to faithfully represent their voices and insights. One way is through multimodal forms of inquiry, such as embedded videos, artwork, and a participatory documentary film co-created by CARE members. These touchstones draw attention to the many people whose knowledge and labor have fueled the research and works against homogenizing their perspectives.

Participatory Documentary

As with other aspects of CBRE, decisions about how to share research involve drawing on the various talents of partnership members. When Dee Asaah, a doctoral student with a background in filmmaking, joined the CARE team, his interest in multimodality dovetailed with prior discussions about research impact and how to reach a broader audience beyond the academy. Dee took the lead on creating, alongside several youth, a participatory documentary on the CARE Initiative. The film *I am Home* (Asaah et al., 2021) contains interviews with community members and footage of them sharing their original research to a variety of audiences. Dee worked closely with a subset of middle and high school youth who had an interest in the arts to plan and execute the filming and involved the whole CARE team dialogically in making decisions about the documentary. Over one summer, under Dee's guidance, youth researchers visited the Catholic parish and neighborhood center to capture the solidarity and joy of their intercultural community. Dee encouraged the youth to pursue their own ideas regarding representation, which led to both technical conversations about angles and approaches to filming specific shots, as well as discussions regarding the history of the church, the experiences of the various cultural and linguistic groups in the parish and surrounding neighborhood, and their shared context of CBRE. The images they took, a subset of which are depicted in Figure 7.1, helped determine the focus of the film. Through their photography and videography, the youth also introduced Dee, who was relatively new to the project, to their own understandings of the site as well as the CARE Initiative. Over the next few years, the youth would themselves take turns with the cameras and microphones, documenting the research process as it was occurring and conducting on-camera interviews with CARE members in the university recording studio (Figures 7.2, 7.3, and 7.4).

We had dedicated community sessions for envisioning the film (see Figure 7.5 for an illustrative agenda), where CARE members reviewed footage, watched excerpts of sample documentaries (e.g., Simon et al., 2017), and deliberated about its content and format. Dee also worked with the Youth

Figure 7.1 Images taken by youth for the documentary. Photos compiled by Dee Asaah.

Figure 7.2 Youth researchers heading to the university recording studio.

Figure 7.3 Youth filming using university equipment.

Figure 7.4 Youth filmmakers.

3. Work groups — 60 mins
- **Documentary Work Group — 30 mins**
  - ○ Show video of the work Dee did with youth during the summer holidays
  - ○ Watch 1 or 2 short docs on community-based research and discuss
  - ○ How might these inform our own docs?
  - ○ What ideas do you have for our doc?
    - ■ Can youth use their cell phones and personal cameras to capture some shots of their communities?
  - ○ Any ideas for music that is representative of our intergen communities?

Figure 7.5 Meeting plans for work sessions on the film.

Research Fellows to review various segments and iterations of the film, make editorial and production decisions, and elicit feedback from the whole group about the provisional choices that had been made. During one small group session, for example, the Research Fellows suggested the need for more opportunities to feature the parents and elders telling their own stories in their native languages. The youth took the lead in interviewing and filming the adults and handled all the translation—composing initial drafts, checking with elders, and fine-tuning the texts to produce the final English subtitles of the film. The goal was to create a documentary everyone literally could see themselves in, and that would authentically reflect our work together. It was a project of collaborative self-definition and self-representation.

Once an initial version of the film was completed, we held a screening at Gerald's university for all the members of the project, which served as a social gathering but also provided an opportunity for everyone to provide feedback for the final edits. The screening—a community "Oscars Night"—was in itself an important component of the film process, not just a means to celebrate with one another all our accomplishments. We opened the evening with a red-carpet arrival to one of the university auditoriums, where members of the partnership posed together for photos and enjoyed dinner before heading to the event. After the screening, a high school youth presented awards to attendees, a lighthearted shout-out to the many people featured in the film whose ongoing investments and labor had helped make the CARE Initiative possible over the years. The documentary was a form of inquiry and a representation of the group's findings. It was also a means to tell a different type of research story, one which highlighted, for example, the affective dimensions of collaborative methods (see Chapter 4) that are hard to convey in traditional academic genres, such as the scholarly article.

Participatory Book Writing

We are also in the process of co-authoring a book provisionally titled *Educational Access and Equity from Families' Perspectives*, which would interweave families' testimonios and their original research on educational access. The book is conceptualized with a practitioner audience in mind, an outgrowth of the families' desires to be in more dialogue with educators. It aims to bring to life the interconnected issues the families have been researching over time paired with responses from educators who have been taking up these ideas in their schools. The group envisions this as a call to action that could be readily engaged with in schools, professional learning communities, and pre-service teaching: an invitation for educators to learn from families in their own respective contexts.

We have been discussing and workshopping the book over the past three years alongside youth and families as we seek to collaboratively determine its scope, content, and format. As part of the participatory composing process, we have conducted an inquiry into how everyone can contribute to the book in a manner that honors their diverse literate repertoires, even if they may not be comfortable with conventional scholarly writing. This process has entailed looking closely and with a critical eye at existing texts for teachers, inquiring into our own purposes for writing the book and how those goals would influence its style, tone, and content, and rethinking the writing process to include multilingualism, community literacies and families' diverse ways of knowing.

Early on in joining the CARE partnership, community educator and organizer Olivia Vazquez Ponce shared her stance on community-based research

Figure 7.6 Olivia presenting research on college access.

with the group, powerfully rendered in her words during a 2019 presentation (see Figure 7.6):

> The process of questioning and changing systems we live within is research.
>   Our community's work toward this doesn't manifest itself in published articles. It manifests in the ways that our communities' lives change.
>   I realized that these ideas need to get published and WE need to be the ones publishing it.

As a community educator with a local immigrant rights organization, Olivia often drew on activist conceptions of research that foregrounded the community's rights to investigate issues that impact their wellbeing. In this presentation, Olivia discussed a reconceptualization of what counts as research from something that outsiders do to practices already occurring amid community-based movements, where researchers are accountable to the larger community itself. The impact of such work, she argued, was not measured by publications alone, but by concrete changes to the inequities such research is seeking to interrupt. While publications are not the primary outcome of research, there is nonetheless an urgency in communicating these ideas. The question then becomes who publishes that work, and Olivia argued for communities' right to publish their own insights: on their terms, in their words, and as aligned to their vision for educational justice.

In community meetings, we have taken time to co-construct the writing process, and to provide multiple creative entry points to convey knowledge in ways that honor composing as more than putting words down on paper. Through workshops and anchoring questions such as those depicted on the sample handout from an intergenerational meeting (Figure 7.7), we have revisited the research findings and educational demands to determine the content partners were most interested in writing about, to generate ideas for the writing practices of the group, and to consider logistics such as time availability.

- Language access: *acceso lingüístico*
- Stopping tracking (AP classes- advanced opportunities for everyone): *clases avanzadas para todos*
- Honoring student cultures and challenging racism: *honrar las culturas de estudiantes e interrumpir el racismo*
- Immigration histories and immigration status: *historias de inmigración y estatus migratorio*
- Family and community involvement: *participación familiar en la educación*
- College access: *Acceso a la universidad*
- Challenging labels and attending to the whole child: *desafiando etiquetas negativas de los estudiantes*
- Mental health and healing: *Salud mental y cómo sanarnos*

Name: _____Contact Information:_____

What I am interested in writing about:

Ideas for how the writing group should run:

Times/days that would work for me to meet:

Anything else you want to tell us:

Figure 7.7 Brainstorming for collaborative book.

This process is a quintessential example of slow scholarship due to two interrelated reasons around community responsiveness: the time-intensive nature of inclusive writing practices, and how shifting priorities have led us to put book writing on the back burner while other concerns or actions are prioritized. For instance, at the workshop where we were utilizing the aforementioned handout in a discussion with parents and community elders, the synthesis of research topics at the top of the page revealed a continued urgency for information about college access. Parents emphasized the need for greater information about the topic and proposed continuing the previous summer's Youth Inquiry into College. While discussions were related to the book-authoring process, for the group writing was not merely about perpetuating academic discourse but rather about ensuring that research and ideas can drive action. These were not competing propositions, since continued inquiry and outreach on the topic would iteratively inform a book chapter on these ideas. Yet we held off on meeting in book groups while other community priorities took precedence.

Writing collaboratively, in ways that honor and uplift the contributions of community members, is not a process to be rushed. We are mindful that schooling practices have often excluded or deficitized low-income communities of color and want to define a new situation of scholarly production where families and youth are valued as genuine partners. This commitment means challenging the ideology of individual authorship and acknowledging that various members will contribute in different but equally important ways. The practices for co-constructing research directions described in Chapter 5 carry over to the collaborative authorship process as we try to think innovatively about translating shared research into a book format, asking questions such as the following: How might oral conversations and the arts be incorporated as a form of composition? How do we braid together different discursive styles and narratives, including across languages? How do we accommodate the fact that some members of the partnership may have more time to dedicate to the writing process, while making sure that everyone is included but not overburdened? How might we envision joyful and generative community-based "writing retreats"?

Collaborative writing, therefore, is not about assimilating community members into a monolithic academic "voice." University-based researchers need to be self-reflexive about whether CBRE, including collaborative writing, is indeed a bidirectional intellectual and creative exchange, or if we are (even subconsciously) trying to forge mini-academics that reproduce standardized genres. All members of a research team can—and do—write in multiple genres, but determining what writing should look like in any given instance is a negotiation about what communication styles and modes best fit the priorities and the intended audience of a piece.

As part of the CARE Initiative's writing inquiries, youth have spent time analyzing existing professional books as potential mentor texts for their own authorial decisions. For example, they created a Jamboard (Figure 7.8) with

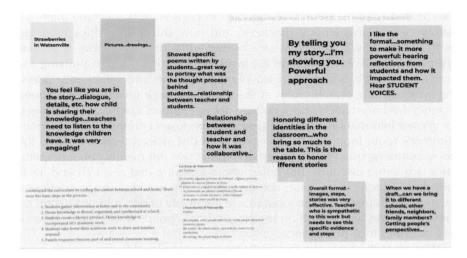

Figure 7.8 Youth researchers' analysis of a professional text for educators.

insights from *Rethinking bilingual education: Welcoming home languages in our classrooms* (Barbian, Gonzales, & Mejía, 2017). This text, like other samples which the youth examined closely, was purposefully selected because it expressed the types of educational justice commitments that members of our partnership had prioritized. As the posted comments indicate, youth appreciated the use of student stories to showcase community knowledge and "honor different identities in the classroom." They also suggested other ways to foreground youth voices, such as "hearing reflections for students and how it impacted them." One group member wondered, "when we have a draft … can we bring it to different schools, other friends, neighbors, family members?" The youth valued additional feedback to ensure multiple viewpoints are included.

The youth also critiqued several of the sample texts. One observation youth and families have raised is about the inaccessibility and esoteric discourse of some academic language, which conveys implicit messages about its intended audience. One youth reflected, "most of these books are made for elites and not created for me … Cover of the book with big words will put off a lot of people." He advocated for a style that communicates "this book is for everybody right from the get go." We are careful, however, about not presuming that more dense theoretical language is not for community researchers. The very youth who raised the critique is a case and point. He has himself, ironically, become quite an intimidating conceptual thinker over the years and plans on attending an elite university in the fall to further his studies in critical theory. But his point was well taken by the whole group, especially because they know, from their own research and lived experiences, that not everyone has access to the language of the academy.

Another critique that community members have raised is that many academic books on educational access assume a white, middle-class audience, irrespective of the author's own identity. One CARE community researcher, for example, was assigned a book when she was studying education in college that spoke directly to her own personal experiences as an immigrant. She commended the general accuracy and quality of the research, but also expressed that it did not offer many new insights to either herself or to members of her community. Her predominantly white peers loved the book and found that its stories provided a window into a world of which they were not familiar. She, however, found the reading of the book and ensuing classroom discussions somewhat voyeuristic and at times difficult because they brought up traumas she had undergone without offering concrete steps for educators to address the injustices that caused them. The CARE Initiative decided, by contrast, that they wanted to write a book for a pluralistic audience, including the community itself, and one that might help make a more immediate intervention.

Going Public as Collective Intellectual Activism

As the examples in this chapter illustrate, significant work goes into thoughtfully orchestrating opportunities for going public with research. It is not just a simple decision to include community members in conference presentations or writing, but a process of engaging *how* this can happen in constructive, caring, and respectful ways that honor the ideals of the partnership. For the members of the CARE Initiative, these ideals include first and foremost viewing research as a form of collective intellectual activism. This means that the dissemination of research ought to dialogically engage and inspire others, that it should lead to action, and that the "products" of research are really just part of the process of inquiry. As the struggle for social and educational justice is ongoing, there are no hard stops for CBRE. We, as a group, keep going as long as we have the will and energy to do so.

As a collectivity of public intellectuals, there is one final form or representation and dissemination of research that the CARE Initiative has begun, but which has not yet come to full fruition. One of our former youth researchers, who went on to study computer science at the university where Gerald works, decided to create a website for the community. More than just an online presence, the website would serve as a digital intellectual commons, a locus of shared resources and a multimedia platform for community knowledge, expression, and social empowerment. The digital commons might be administered or stewarded by individuals, but it would thrive on the knowledge and resources generated from the community and would be for the community.

On the one hand, the digital commons would provide an archive for all the research that the CARE Initiative has done over the years, and more time encased projects—such as the documentary, book, research artifacts—could be housed on the site. As new generations become interested in college access, for example, they could learn from the work the community has already done in that area. It could also be a space to preserve local history, store and curate pictures and other primary records of the neighborhood, including the history and legacy of the CARE Initiative itself. This preservation is important, especially in the face of predatory development and community displacement. On the other hand, the digital commons would also be a living form of scholarly representation, always in the act of becoming, much like the organic nature of the community itself. Community members would be able to edit and update the site through democratic, open-access processes. The possibilities for creative forms of intellectual and scholarly expression are expansive and seemingly endless (vlogs, daily journals, photovoice projects, etc.), ideally encompassing a multiplicity of community voices across generations, languages, and cultural and racialized experiences.

Our website is not up yet, and we have more to learn from our colleagues, in the community and university alike, who have expertise on digital platforms (e.g. Nichols & Stornaiuolo, 2019). Like so many aspects of the CARE Initiative, we have been improvising as we go to adapt to changing circumstances, grounded in the history of our partnership and guided by our shared commitments. What we have learned, however, is that there are many vistas of possibility for representing our collective labor and engaging in intellectual activism.

Questions for Reflection

1. Who is the audience for your community-based research?
2. How will the research be shared and disseminated in a manner that promotes dialogue and action?
3. How might authorship and representation be creatively reimagined to accommodate the collective?

References

Asaah, D., Campano, G., & Ghiso, M. P., with youth and families from the CARE Initiative (2021). *I am home: A partnership for better education* (Documentary film). Philadelphia, PA.

Barbian, E., Gonzales, G. C., & Mejía, P. (Eds.). (2017). *Rethinking bilingual education: Welcoming home languages in our classrooms*. Rethinking Schools.

Nichols, T. P., & Stornaiuolo, A. (2019). Assembling "digital literacies": Contingent pasts, possible futures. *Media & Communication, 7*(2), 14–24.

Simon, R. (Producer), Baer, P. (Director), with Evis, S., Walkland, T., hicks, b.l., and teachers and youth in the Addressing Injustices Project (2017). *Gender is like an ocean*. (Documentary film). Toronto, ON. http://addressinginjustices.com

Thakurta, A., Kannan, C., Moon, J., & Ghiso, M. P. (2021). A seat at the table: Preparing youth to shape institutional change at an NCTE roundtable presentation. *Voices from the Middle, 28*(4), 69–74.

8 What Is the Impact of CBRE?

Individual and Collective Self-Determination

To understand the impact of CBRE, it is necessary to sketch the background conditions which make it both an epistemologically valuable and a politically urgent methodology. The youth and families in the CARE Initiative, for example, live in the most impoverished large city in the country, and this economic precarity is reflected in their education. During our time during the project, families have endured the shuttering of neighborhood schools due to severe budget cuts at the state level. Children were thus uprooted from the educational communities and teachers with whom they had developed trusting relationships and reassigned to overcrowded schools across the city. Many students are trying to learn in buildings with damaged asbestos, flaking lead paint, mold, flooding, rodent infestations, poor ventilation, and other environmental hazards. Schools do not have adequate air-conditioning systems. As the youth researchers in the CARE Initiative have documented, the material infrastructure of schooling is literally sickening students and their teachers. The asthma rate in the city is nearly double the national average, yet there are schools that do not have nurses. Teachers often spend hundreds of their own dollars on school supplies.

Despite these conditions, the students and their families remain committed to the promise of schooling and have expressed gratitude to many of their teachers and school leaders whom they see as advocates. Yet their aspirations are also undercut by a system that provides inadequate access to higher education and beyond. The school district and many of the charter schools are underfunded. There are schools without arts programs and ones that do not offer precalculus to their high school students, or other advanced placement courses. The school district has significantly more police than counselors. This fact alone speaks to how the criminalization of Black, Brown, and immigrant youth and their families has become naturalized in a society that invests more in the carceral state than in fundamental human well-being.

While we sketch the conditions of our city, they are not unique. We imagine that many readers of this book are aware of similar conditions in their own respective sites of research and practice. As critical social theorists have recently argued, the dispossession, displacement, surveillance, and

DOI: 10.4324/9781003279686-8

exploitation of marginalized communities has become a totalizing system, leading to a racialized global order in many ways akin to apartheid (Besterman, 2020). These systemic injustices are, to put it bluntly, the default impact of the status quo, of not doing anything. Education researchers concerned with inequality often create interventions meant to make a difference within their respective areas of expertise, interventions whose impact can be measured. For example, as literacy scholars, we might develop approaches to reading and writing instruction that may lead to increased test scores. This is, of course, potentially important work, as all the families we know want their children to improve their reading. Supporting students in their literacy skills has indeed been an integral part of the CARE Initiative since its inception. From the perspective of CBRE, however, the improvement of discrete skills frames the problem too narrowly and, very often, from the vantage point of those in power.

Top-down educational interventions may be beneficial to individual students, but they do not holistically support communities. And they fail to fundamentally challenge the baseline policies and practices emerging from and reproducing axes of multiple forms of oppression. The families in the CARE Initiative certainly want their children to be able to read proficiently, but ultimately what they desire is an intellectually and creatively engaging curriculum that honors their children's brilliance and enhances their life opportunities (see demands in Chapter 6). Given the aforementioned conditions, however, the net effect of these skills-based interventions with quantifiable objectives is an education system that primarily remediates students, giving them the "basic" skills to ultimately contribute to a service economy as a tractable and precarious low-wage labor force. This renewed emphasis on discrete skills is occurring during an authoritarian period in the United States, in reaction to the 2020 uprisings for Black lives, which is attempting to stifle critical thought through the banning of books and ideas, such as those that address structural racism or reflect LGBTQAI+ identities. As many have noted, the system may be functioning just as it has been designed: to reinforce the ideology of the dominant majority and reproduce social stratification along intersectional axes of race, immigration status, class, and gender. Fortunately, we live in a city that has longstanding intellectual and activist legacies of resistance and critical educators both within and outside of the schools.

CBRE as an Alternative to the Dominant Default

At the risk of hyperbolism, we would argue that, from the perspective of CBRE, the real problem is existential: It is about the very existence of communities as they struggle to sustain their livelihoods and, ideally, thrive under conditions of entrenched inequality. We risk this claim because we believe the historical record cannot be denied, despite political efforts to do so in education. The oppression of Black, Indigenous, and people of color (BIPOC) communities, originating in the foundational genocides of the enslavement of Africans, the theft of Indigenous lands, and imperial wars and colonization, have taken on new permutations that impact the quotidian realities of communities. Families we have worked with in the CARE Initiative, for example, have been caught up in ICE raids and sent to detention centers, lost loved ones due to inadequate health care, been displaced from their homes because of gentrification, and have had their labor exploited in racialized and gendered work sectors.

CBRE is one response to these realities that builds off the hope that many families and communities place in education. Like all research approaches, CBRE will invariably be imperfect and certainly does not have all the answers. Educational inequities are wrought with contradiction, especially for those who navigate them daily, including teachers, students, and families (Simon & Campano, 2013). CBRE does presuppose that in a community of inquiry, members might learn from one another and co-create knowledge about how to make education better and, in the process, more fully realize on their own terms a shared and ever-evolving vision of educational justice. It is about researching from the thick of things, from the complex realities of one's lived experiences. What distinguishes CBRE is that it offers an alternative paradigm of research and social organization from the dominant default, one that is cultivated from the bottom up. It strives to create conditions for new kinds of questions that are not defined by those in power, critiquing systemic policies and practices that erode communities and promoting values that may not be measurable by conventional education metrics. In the process, it may also prefigure more holistic and organic educational arrangements where community members have greater agency in shaping their realities.

Impact as Individual and Collective Self-Determination

We suggest that the impact of CBRE is one of individual and collective self-determination. This finding is the result of qualitative evidence we have collected on the CARE Initiative, and which can be understood through a series of nested concentric circles (Figure 8.1). The innermost circle is how involvement in CBRE impacts individuals. These individuals, of course, cannot be separated from the more immediate community of researchers who have been regularly involved in the project over the years. This core group, of roughly 30–40 family members and 15 or so university-based researchers, would be reflected by the second circle radiating from the center. The third circle speaks to the impact that the CARE Initiative has had on those more tangentially related to the project, including those who have been able to participate online as part of a broader virtual community. And the final outermost circle refers to the ways in which CBRE is both nourished by and nourishes larger social movements for justice.

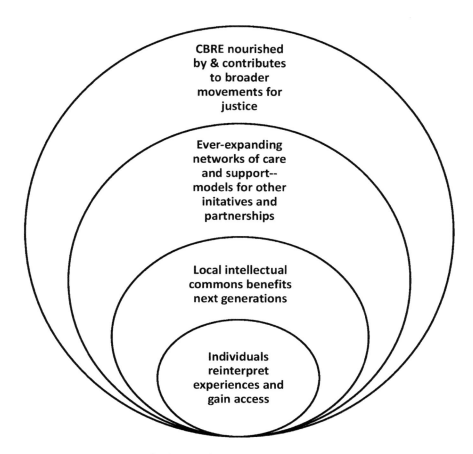

Figure 8.1 CBRE's nested spheres of impact.

First Sphere of Impact: Promoting Individual Flourishing

Our research has always foregrounded issues of educational access. From the very beginning community leaders in the partnership have stated that education is what gives their community hope and we have repeated to the youth that institutions of higher education, such as those with whom we are affiliated, would be lucky to have any of them as students. Over the past decade the CARE Initiative has conducted sustained participatory research on the high school admissions process (Yee, Mostafa, & Campano, 2016), for example, as well as the college application process (Ghiso et al., 2022). The youth have also conducted significant original research which they have shared in scholarly journals and at conferences, in the process demystifying academia. As one of the CARE youth stated: "I used to think scholars and researchers were way up there, on another planet, but through our work I realized that I am a researcher."

There is ample evidence that the CARE Initiative has played a role in helping to provide educational access for individuals. For example, just about all the youth who have been part of CARE Initiative in a sustained manner have been accepted to, and have chosen to attend, various colleges and universities, including the University of Pennsylvania, Temple, Penn State, Yale, University of Pittsburgh, Swarthmore, Princeton, Community College of Philadelphia, and Wesleyan, to name a few. It is important to underscore, however, that the partnership is not simply about access to higher education. It is about sustaining the conditions for both individual and community survival and flourishing, which for any person may or may not involve postsecondary education. And, importantly, once a youth enters adulthood, they will always be part of the CARE Initiative if they so choose.

We are anticipating some of the next rings of impact because it is indeed hard to separate individual from collective flourishing, but what we suggest is that, on a fundamental psychological level, one of the most important impacts of CBRE is that it provides a collaborative space for individuals to (re)interpret their experiences in more empowering ways. Individuals harness the knowledge generated from the research community to reframe their experiences so as not to internalize a sense of failure from not having adequately conformed to external standards and metrics of success. They transform their personal struggles into a collective commitment to systemic change.

For example, one of the youth, Miguel, expressed disappointment and frustration when he realized that he may not be taking enough advanced placement (AP) courses. He had an inchoate sense that this was the result of something not fair, but nonetheless felt personal inadequacy. When Miguel, along with several peers, conducted an initial inquiry into tracking, they discovered that Latine and other students of color were severely underrepresented in AP courses, and this was the result of implicit racism, not individual failure. In their research, the youth exposed how one's ability to access to AP opportunities was tied to scores on a qualifying exam, the lack of clarity about the scheduling and the content of the tests, the variation across of departmental practices about who or who is not admitted to AP within the same school, and the racial disparities of higher tracked courses (Campano et al., 2022). Tracking was eventually selected as one of the youth researchers' priorities for further inquiry. Students documented how accessing AP courses took place at their respective schools, interviewed youth and families about their experiences, reflected on their own testimonials, and read current research on the topic. Their goal was to paint an analytic portrait of how these tracking mechanisms work on the ground, often in contrast to stated equity goals, and recommend changes in school practice.

When presenting their research at an education conference, the youth reported how teacher recommendations impact access to course offerings.

Byron, another Latine high schooler, expanded on the role of bias and race in education, noting, "Everyone has biases but not everyone is aware of these exactly … And something we have noticed while doing research is that students of color will be less likely to get a recommendation from a teacher that is not of color." Lukas, a youth researcher of Indonesian descent, added,

> We have also found that White students who are taught by White teachers are twice as likely to get recommended into a gifted program at their school, and if Black children are taught by Black teachers, the ratio is that they are just as likely to be admitted as white students.

Miguel thus developed his understanding of tracking and AP courses in concert with his peers as part of a supportive interpretive community. Together, they shifted the discourse from individual deficit to systemic critique. Miguel redirected his feelings of alienation and internalized inadequacy into righteous indignation and a desire for advocacy—individual advocacy for his own spot in an AP course but also broader advocacy in meeting with his principal and calling for a review of the racial disparities of tracking in his school.

Dee, in his work as part of the CARE Initiative as well as his own CBRE dissertation study (Asaah, 2021), explicitly invited members of the research team to inquire into what constitutes "success." One of the immigrant mothers in CARE had expressed sadness that her life was not conforming to dominant definitions of the "American Dream": in particular, the hegemonic idea that somehow one's worth can be measured in dollars. As part of her inquiry into success with Dee and other CARE members, she came to realize that in fact she had been remarkably successful in life. She and her family had survived sectarian violence in their home country and had created a meaningful life in our city, supporting future generations to have more life opportunities, despite significant challenges. Because of his own transnational experiences as being from a minoritized community both in his home country and in the United States, Dee was in a unique position to help the mother understand just how remarkable she was as a parent and community leader and why she was a hero in so many of our eyes.

Several of us in the CARE Initiative who are either faculty or graduate students have, in turn, benefited from the collective interpretations of our larger research community. We do not stand outside the community research but are part of it and benefit from its impact as well. Despite the privilege of being from the university, academia has, seemingly, endless ways of communicating that we are not doing enough or are not enough, sometimes resurfacing feelings of imposter syndrome. This may be especially the case for research that engages communities, which is often coded as service. Of relevance here is C. Thi Nguyen's understanding of value collapse: the ways in which institutions pressure individuals to conform to a value system not of their own making (RoyIntPhilosophy, 2022).

As we discussed in Chapter 3, many students enter doctoral studies because of their deeply held values and a dedication to educational transformation. Often their motivation stems from their own personal experiences with schooling, as students and/or teachers, where they have witnessed, first-hand, unconscionable inequities in the school system. Although all the details may not be fully fleshed out, they imagine for themselves a serious, long-term commitment to working in solidarity with children, youth, and families in the service of education justice. For many of them it is not just about getting a job but about tailoring one's life project through research. Once in the institutional context of academia, however, this complex and nuanced vision of a meaningful life in educational research and practice, what our mentor Susan L. Lytle often referred to as one's "work in the world," becomes translated into explicit and reductive institutional metrics for success, such as publication records, impact factors, rankings, awards, grants, exclusive scholarly clubs, and so on. When these metrics become too much of an obsession, they serve as a stand-in for more robustly qualitative and subtle understandings of one's work and life. At worst, they might lead to a kind of value collapse or even elite capture (Táíwò, 2022).

The community-based researchers have helped us keep our work grounded on what matters and to counteract or mitigate value fade. For example, while reflecting on a scholarly presentation by our youth that induced a collective sense of awe among the research team and audience alike, one of our elders, Daria, stated that "this is the real work, not the typical BS of people who just come and take from the community." Her words were a comment on researchers and others who employ extractivist methodologies for professional gain. The community researchers keep us in check. They encourage us when we are on the right track, but also remind us to be vigilant about value fade: to not lose sight of what brought us into the field of education in the first place or become distracted by professional competition or opportunism.

One of the promises and impacts of CBRE is that people hermeneutically have one another's backs, which we believe is a form of collective intellectual care work that reinforces social bonds of empathy and solidarity, often across boundaries of language, race, class, and institution. Individuals are invited to understand their experiences from multiple perspectives informed by collaborative research. This kind of community-sourcing of interpretation shifts who controls the narrative of one's own educational and life experiences. Individuals mobilize the knowledge of the community to counteract systemic inequities and external metrics to create their own more cogent and empowering narratives. The new narrative could be of a high school student who transforms feelings of inadequacy into one of advocacy, a doctoral student who refuses to shed their previous identity as a teacher or community organizer in order to live the academy on their own terms, or a parent who redefines the American Dream to be less about individual upward mobility and more about community survival and thriving. These examples, and so many more we have documented over the years, illustrate forms of self-determination nourished by the relational and interdependent scholarly ethos of CBRE.

Second Sphere of Impact: Cultivating a Grassroots Intellectual Commons

Individual participants benefit from CBRE, but the relationship between the individual and the larger community is reciprocal. Individuals contribute to the larger scholarly and intellectual culture of which they are a part. They research and create diverse forms of knowledge for the betterment of society. While we understand CBRE as a form of participatory justice, we reject the idea that it is preparing youth, or families, to become "productive members of society" because too often it is society itself which is the problem, as revealed, for example, by our youths' inquiry into state-sanctioned racialized violence in their own city and beyond (Ghiso et al., 2022; Staufert-Reyes et al., 2022). When we ask ourselves what has enabled our own project to sustain itself and why would families navigating extremely challenging circumstances—for example, as essential workers or as students in an under-resourced school district—to continue to engage in participatory inquiry, we keep returning to the same answer: the fundamental human capacity and creative desire to collaboratively generate knowledge around issues of justice that directly impact one's community. Because of the intergenerational and long-term nature of the project, the families in the CARE Initiative have cultivated a local scholarly legacy based on their collective research, creating a grassroots' intellectual commons from which to draw continued inspiration and insight. We use the word "commons" because the knowledge generated by CBRE is open and available to anyone who has the passion to participate, and it aspires to be shared and stewarded democratically. It is grassroots because the research arises organically from the inquiries of the community members themselves.

This collective knowledge of the commons has more traditional academic manifestations, such as scholarly publications and presentations. This is no surprise because many in the group are affiliated with universities and schools. They have also included several other creative ways of representing and sharing the work, such as the stories elders pass down to younger generations, memories of traveling and presenting at scholarly conferences, an accumulative conceptual vocabulary to name and analyze injustices, a list of educational demands derived from the research, photo documentation and inquiry, and a participatory documentary of our work together (see Chapter 7). The participants also draw from and contribute knowledge from their involvement in social formations outside the project, including from their participation in activist collectivities, neighborhood organizations, online communities, and schooling.

Over the past few years, a cornerstone of our intellectual commons has been the role of Research Fellows, youth who have been involved in the project for years and now play a leadership role both on the university team and community side of the project. The Fellows, in many ways, embody the project. One former Fellow declared "I literally have spent half my life in the project." Another, a recent university graduate, has been involved since he immigrated to the United States from Indonesia, and the one-time youngest member of the CARE Initiative who joined the partnership in kindergarten is now a senior in high school and a Fellow herself. The Fellows are keepers of the historical memory of the project and serve as invaluable role models for younger generations. These newer generations are rarely novices to CBRE. Some were siblings, cousins, and friends who, as younger children, may have been on the periphery of the research but nonetheless absorbed the culture of inquiry osmotically. Others have participated in kindred community-based organizations, which have a similar ethos of inquiry and have engaged in many of the same social justice topics (Rusoja, 2022). Even individuals from neighboring towns have heard about the work of the project. For example, a Vietnamese high school student from a predominately white suburb of the city, but with roots in South Philly, reached out to us because he had read an article published by one of our youth researchers and wanted to be part of an intellectual community that could help him grapple with the resurgence of anti-Asian violence. His affluent independent school did not provide him or his peers of color with the space and resources to make sense of what he and his family were enduring, a hermeneutic injustice (Fricker, 2007) which compelled him to seek an alternative scholarly and social community.

One advantage of such a robust, local intellectual commons is that we are never beginning from scratch. Many of our inquiries are ongoing and build off previous work. For example, for years, members of the research team have been investigating interracial solidarity and anti-Black racism (e.g., Campano et al., 2016; Ghiso et al., 2020, 2022; Player, 2018). These were legacies of inquiry in which current members of the project were either directly or indirectly involved. Therefore, when the youth decided to examine the rise of hate crimes during the pandemic or anti-Black racism in the aftermath of George Floyd's murder, they were intellectually and emotionally better prepared to engage in this difficult work than they would have been if this were a short-term project. Because they were part of a community-based intellectual commons, the youth's self-assurance as scholars and knowledge-generators is not dependent on their schooling experiences.

Third Sphere of Impact: Expanding Networks of Care and Belonging

Another form of impact is that the families have created expanding networks of belonging and care. Inspired by the disability justice movement, we understand collective care work as a "practical survival strategy" but also a process of "community and political organizing" (Piepzna-Samarasinha, 2018, p. 45). While we began as an intentionally-formed research and educational support community, we developed, over time, into a broader network of care and belonging. Miguel, a youth member who is currently in college, recalled joining the group when he was in eighth grade and what it has meant for him:

> I just loved how welcoming the group was. Like, as soon as I got there, I made a lot of friends. Everyone was very, very nice … they welcomed me like they already knew me. That's what I love. Like Gerald and María Paula are saying, time flies, it feels like I just joined literally yesterday, and now I am a Fellow and I am helping facilitate things. I just recently helped [then-doctoral student] Ankhi plan a lesson and you know I just love working with everyone. I get to learn a lot from other people. I get to share what I know, and I just love expanding my knowledge and keep hearing everyone's different points of view … I think [the group] it's just very welcoming. It's like a family and they, the people have been there for me from the start.

As Miguel's comments suggest, the scholarly inquiries that the group undertake are occurring within the caring relationships that make the group a chosen "family." For many individuals, this network helps make the research feel like an extension of the care work of their everyday lives, rather than an additional task or responsibility on top of everything else. Many people who have become involved in the partnership have done so organically through already established relationships. And involvement in the project has helped foster new relational bonds, which in turn generate new possibilities for social and intellectual organizing. These bonds and possibilities may traverse the globe. For instance, in her dissertation research Ankhi Thakurta brought together Indonesian youth from the CARE Initiative with youth from Calcutta, India to investigate, as a transnational community of inquiry, urban migrant girlhoods. In this way, we understand the CARE Initiative as one node in an ever-expanding and evolving network of care and support.

The interrelations among various members of the group are illustrative of these rhizomatic networks. For example, when Alicia Rusoja was a doctoral working on the project, she introduced us to Olivia Vazquez Ponce, a community leader who had organized with a local immigrant rights organization, with whom Alicia was doing her own dissertation research (Rusoja, 2017). Olivia would eventually work alongside Chloe Kannan, then a doctoral student, and an undergraduate student to support a summer collaborative inquiry into college with a group of roughly 28 high school students from throughout Philadelphia, including longstanding CARE Initiative members as well as other young people who had heard about the research project through our networks. The group met regularly at the university throughout the summer. The facilitators shared their extensive knowledge as scholars and organizers, including several of their experiences as first-generation college students with DACA status who were navigating higher education. Chloe, the lead facilitator, designed the collaborative inquiry around critical literacy and youth participatory action research, which would also later inform her own dissertation research on college access (Kannan, 2021). The youth presented their original research to their own families as well as to a packed crowd at the Penn Annual Ethnography and Education Forum, on topics such the cost of a university education, improving campus climate for students of color, and the interconnections between mental health and academic thriving. When Olivia herself transferred from Community College to Swarthmore, she created her own program on demystifying college access with her Swarthmore peers for new generations of Philadelphia high school students. Gerald gave a guest talk to the program and met Zenith, one of the participants. Zenith would eventually join the CARE Initiative himself, becoming a Research Fellow and staying involved throughout his years as a university student at Penn State, supporting younger generations around issues of college access and equity.

Even after accepting academic positions in California, Alicia sustained relationships she had cultivated as a graduate student. At community members' request, including Olivia who continues to work as an educator/ organizer/scholar, she expanded the collaborative research to focus on the impact of Covid-19 on the political organizing, education, and grassroots research practice of Latine/x immigrants during and post the pandemic. And Chloe has returned to her own Anishinaabe community to help develop The Indigenous Education Youth Collective (IEYC), a research-practice partnership between two public universities and Anishinaabe youth to center indigenous ways of knowing, revitalize community knowledge that has been lost, and allow students to better connect with their Native identities while navigating educational spaces. Chloe too continues to support youth in Philadelphia in pursuing their own higher education aspirations.

We go into a little detail about just one of the relational networks to provide a concrete sense of the kind of social capital individuals inherit when they become part of the chosen family of the CARE Initiative. A young person, for example, may not have immediate family members who have gone to college. Through CBRE, however, they develop meaningful and trusting relations with many individuals who have navigated higher education and beyond, including with previous youth members who have done research on educational access and with university students, many of whom are scholars of color and first-generation themselves. White university students who have grown up in segregated white neighborhoods, but who aspire to work in solidarity with communities of color in the city, have been mentored by community elders, such as Daria, into how to do so ethically and in a manner that does not perpetuate savior ideologies. But the value of the networks goes beyond one's educational and professional goals. Over the years individuals in the CARE Initiative have celebrated life milestones, grieved at funerals together, visited one another in hospitals, supported one another in political actions, and have shared many meals in a spirit of congregation and mutual care.

Fourth Sphere of Impact: Participating in Movements for Social Justice

Another example of a relational network illustrates our final sphere of impact, how CBRE is both shaped by but may also contribute to broader social justice movements. This network can be traced to Mary Yee, who as a doctoral student, worked with the CARE Initiative in its early years. Mary entered the program after decades of experience as an educator in the school district and a community organizer. She was a founding member of a grassroots community-based organization, Asian Americans United, and was actively involved in protecting Philadelphia's Chinatown from the damaging effects of large-scale building projects for decades from the 1970s. With the CARE Initiative, Mary helped to facilitate participatory action research with parents from the Indonesian community around the Philadelphia school district's high school admissions process (Yee et al., 2016). Mary's own dissertation would eventually become a longitudinal case study of Asian American youth activists in the city (Yee, 2018).

One of the community researchers with whom Mary worked alongside in the CARE Initiative is Ivy's mother. When Ivy entered high school, she became interested in researching the Chinatown neighborhood, the role it plays for its residents and well as the broader Asian community in our city, and its current struggle to combat predatory development with the proposed building of an athletic stadium immediately adjacent to the neighborhood. Ivy and other youth studied collaborative and dialogical research methods as they grappled with what it means to learn about other people's communities (they of course had experience with researchers, including ourselves, learning about their own South Philly neighborhood) by interviewing Chinatown residents, leaders, and elders. Ivy also accepted an internship with Asian Americans United. Her interest in Chinatown connected deeply with a doctoral student in the CARE Initiative, Claire So, who has roots in New York City's Chinatown communities, as well as an undergraduate student activist who grew up in Philadelphia. When they began to learn more about Chinatown, they themselves took important organizing roles in the movement to save the neighborhood, working shoulder to shoulder with longtime community leaders. They demonstrate that an important part of knowing about the world involves knowing how to change it for the better and view their research as inseparable from their organizing.

A potential impact of CBRE is that it contributes to broader movements for social justice, where individuals begin to understand themselves as part of collective ongoing legacies of resistance. These movements are often not solely about the interests of a specific community, although this is of primary importance, but have more universal resonance as well. For example, through their research and work alongside the Chinatown movement, Ivy, Claire and other CARE Initiative members have met organizers from across the city who are defending their own neighborhoods from gentrification and fighting for housing justice, which they understand as a human right. They are showing up for one another, across social and community boundaries and in a spirit of solidarity. Going back to the first circle of impact, we can see the ways in which community members' inquiries into the "dense particularities" (Mohanty, 1995, p. 94) of their own subjective experiences may lead to more objective understanding of their shared world and how it may be transformed through collective organizing and action.

Toward Participatory Justice in Education

CBRE is a precarious form of research for precarious times, and perhaps is more urgent for being so. It is one important scholarly vehicle for intellectual organizing and direct democracy, and, as we have argued, for advancing epistemic rights of all people. The researchers in the CARE Initiative exercise their epistemic rights through a variety of knowledge projects across different scales, but they also demand that their research has uptake in concrete settings as a form of action. Throughout this book we hope to have demonstrated how the CARE Initiative collectively embodies an understanding of research and decision-making that goes well beyond the typical calls to "include community voices" to a more robust vision of participatory justice in education. We have learned from the CARE Initiative that participatory justice is not realized in a moment in time, such as a conference or a meeting with a school leader, but it is an ongoing intellectual and relational labor: conducting the research itself; preparing to present the research to a range of audiences, including in contexts where families have historically and constitutively been excluded; fighting to make sure that the research is productively taken up in a manner that leads to change; and following up on promises and plans to ensure that they are not just words. For many families in the CARE Initiative, participatory justice means bringing others on board to their collective knowledge and action projects, including teachers, school leaders, university-based researchers, and all educators who work with students across their lifespans in a spirit of care and solidarity.

We have been humbled and edified by the families' collective agency as they generate knowledge about educational access and equity and engage multiple audiences with their research. We realize that change will most likely not be initiated by those in power. It should not be the burden, however, of families and communities to do all the work. Institutions, such as schools and universities, need to dismantle their exclusionary structures and figure out how they can better learn from and alongside communities. We call on all readers of this book to imagine better ways to advance epistemic rights and participatory justice in their own respective contexts of research, practice, and action.

In our concluding chapter, we end with testimonials of members from the CARE Initiative about what conducting research has meant for them.

Questions for Reflection

1. How do community members measure and understand the impact of their research?
2. What is the relationship between an individual's work in CBRE and the work of the larger group and community?
3. How can members of the partnership better ensure that community research is productively taken up by different audiences, including educators, policy makers, and others in positions of power?
4. How do community members embrace their own power?

References

Asaah, D. (2021). *"The target doesn't matter if the journey wasn't fun": A multimodal exploration of multiplicity and success with transnational youth and their tutors at a community-based organization* (Publication No. 28712785) [Doctoral Dissertation, University of Pennsylvania]. ProQuest Dissertations Publishing.

Besterman, C. (2020). *Militarized global apartheid*. Duke University Press.

Campano, G., Ghiso, M. P., & Thakurta, A. (2022). Community-based partnerships: Fostering epistemic rights through improvement focused research. In D. Peurach, J. L. Russell, L. Cohen-Vogel, & W. R. Penuel (Eds.), *Foundational handbook on improvement-focused educational research* (pp. 189–210). Rowan & Littlefield.

Campano, G., Ngo, L., Low, D. E., & Jacobs, K. B. (2016). Young children demystifying and remaking the university through critical play. *Journal of Early Childhood Literacy, 16*(2), 199–227.

Fricker, M. (2007). *Epistemic injustice: Power and the ethics of knowing*. Oxford University Press.

Ghiso, M. P., Campano, G., Player, G., Krishanwongso, B., & Gultom, F. (2020). Braiding stories toward a common cause: Coalitional inquiry and activism. In V. Kinloch, T. Burkhard, & C. Penn (Eds.), *Race, justice, and activism in literacy instruction* (pp. 181–200). Teachers College Press.

Ghiso, M. P., Campano, G., Thakurta, A., & Vazquez Ponce, O. (2022). Community-based research with immigrant families: Sustaining an intellectual commons of care, resistance, and solidarity in an urban intensive context. *Urban Education* [online first], https://doi.org/10.1177/00420859221082676

Kannan, C. A. (2021). *A critical inquiry into college: Critical literacy in a college readiness program for first-generation students of color* (Publication No. 28645371) [Doctoral Dissertation, University of Pennsylvania]. ProQuest Dissertations Publishing.

Mohanty, C. T. (1995). Feminist encounters: Locating the politics of experience. In L. Nicholson & S. Seidman (Eds.), *Social postmodernism: Beyond identity politics* (pp. 68–86). Cambridge University Press.

Piepzna-Samarasinha, L. L. (2018). *Care work: Dreaming disability justice*. Arsenal Pulp Press.

Player, G. D. (2018). *Unnormal sisterhood: Girls of color writing, reading, resisting, and being together* (Publication No. 10843763) [Doctoral Dissertation, University of Pennsylvania]. ProQuest Dissertations Publishing.

RoyIntPhilosophy (2022). C. Thi Nguyen: "Value collapse"—The Royal Institute of Philosophy Cardiff Annual Lecture 2022 [Video]. YouTube. www.youtube.com/watch?v=zt03qjTyefU

Rusoja, A. (2017). *We are our own best advocates: Latinx immigrants teaching and learning for their rights* (Publication No. 10273554) [Doctoral Dissertation, University of Pennsylvania]. ProQuest Dissertations Publishing.

Rusoja, A. (2022). "Our community is filled with experts": The critical intergenerational literacies of Latinx immigrants that facilitate a communal pedagogy of resistance. *Research in the Teaching of English, 56*(3), 301–327.

Simon, R., & Campano, G. (2013). Activist literacies: Teacher research as resistance to the "normal curve." *Journal of Language and Literacy Education, 9*(1), 21–39.

Staufert-Reyes, E., Wan, C., Thakurta, A., Winch, J. Sikes, Z., Luong, Q., & Ghiso, M. P. (2022). Cultivating virtual communities of care: Reflections on community-based research in times of precarity. *Literacy Research: Theory, Method, and Practice, 71*(1), 437–459.

Táíwò, O. O. (2022). *Elite capture: How the powerful took over identity politics (and everything else)*. Haymarket Books.

Yee, M. P. (2018). *Transformative trajectories of first-generation immigrant youth activists* (Publication No. 10840716). [Doctoral Dissertation, University of Pennsylvania]. ProQuest Dissertations Publishing.

Yee, M., Mostafa, K., & Campano, G. (2016). Participatory research with parents: Mobilizing social capital to support children's education. In G. Campano, M. P. Ghiso, & B. J. Welch, *Partnering with immigrant communities: Action through literacy* (pp. 39–53). Teachers College Press.

9 Community Perspectives on CBRE

This book has been written from the perspective of two university-based researchers in the dialogical consultation with community members. To close, we would like to share testimonials from community members themselves about what community-based research has meant to them.

Mi nombre es María Hernández, soy parte de esta investigación colaborativa. El propósito y esperanza es ser vistos y escuchados, obtener conexión, un lazo mutuo, para tener mejores oportunidades educativas, mejores mensajes. Ofrecer apoyo al estudiante, darle confianza, seguridad y oportunidad de expresión. Tener empatía, mostrar que nos importan sus sentimientos. No subestimar al estudiante. No minimizarlo. No mostrar que solo vale una letra o un número. No etiquetas. No estereotipos. Los estudiantes también son maestros.

Caminemos unidos como seres humanos. Nadie puede solo, todos necesitamos de todos. Caminemos juntos, un paso a la vez, por un mejor futuro equitativo y justo. Somos parte del mismo universo, todos tenemos la llave mágica para unirnos. No seas tú quien cierre este lazo, mejoremos juntos para mejores generaciones. Gracias por la oportunidad.

[My name is María Hernández, I am part of this collaborative research.

The purpose and hope is to be seen and heard, to gain connection, a mutual bond, to have better educational opportunities, better messages. To offer support to the students, give them confidence, security, and opportunities for expression. To have empathy, show that we care about their feelings. To not underestimate students. To not minimize them. To not show that only a letter or number is valid. No labels. No stereotypes. Students are teachers too.

Let's walk together as human beings. No one can do it alone, we all need everyone.

Let us walk together, one step at a time, for a better, equitable, and just future. We are part of the same universe, we all have the magic key to unite us. Don't be the one to close this bond, let's improve together for better generations. Thank you for the opportunity.]

– María Hernández, community leader and parent to two children

DOI: 10.4324/9781003279686-9

Communities Advancing Research Education (CARE) was started with a multi-ethnic group at St. Thomas Aquinas in South Philadelphia, with members from the Black, Indonesian, Latino, and Vietnamese communities. The professors and doctoral students showed us that some educators truly care about our concerns regarding the importance of our children's education and futures. Topics addressed at our monthly meetings included bullying, language barriers, and misinterpretation of information.

Since 2011, with the help of Professors Gerald Campano and María Paula Ghiso and their doctoral students, we have traveled and given our voices, with solutions, to conferences in Washington DC, New York, Baltimore, and here in Pennsylvania. We became a family, a team who really cares about the welfare of all of our children. The doctoral students have been anchors for our children, helping them develop the curricula that best suit them and understand the schools that best serve them. Our children have flourished and realized the benefits of solidarity, being there for each other's causes.

Through this journey of growth, discovery, and confidence, the majority of our students have gone to college. They have become amazingly gifted and caring individuals who are now mentors and are going to go and make good things happen.

– Daria Ward, founder of the Concerned Black Catholics of St. Thomas Aquinas

Community-based research, while sounding like a mouthful, is something every person can find a home in. I have been a part of the CARE project since 6th grade and in my many years, I have learned that community-based research is a journey that each individual takes on their own. The CARE project created a space where I could look into my multiple identities and communities such as being a Philadelphian, Indonesian-American, coming from a low-income background, and being a student, and understand the ways that my community can be strengthened. Within the project, I have worked alongside my peers on projects understanding educational inequity in Philadelphia, understanding questions of access in the college application system, and understanding the role of multinational and intergenerational communities in education. The project also gave me a support group to conduct independent work such as conducting a qualitative research project on the impacts of Covid-19 on Asian American youth in Philadelphia. Beyond just research, the CARE project has given my family and me a community that we know stands alongside us. Amid the struggles and turbulence of the present, the project has taught me that one of the most powerful forces is solidarity. I owe so much of my current accomplishments and future success to the amazing support of the CARE project. I would not be who I am today without this group.

– Owen Setiawan, youth researcher

CARE started for me when I was just about seven years old. The penpal initiative had started my journey with CARE. My pen pal and I conversed a lot about our stationery loves, and she used to send me sticker pages with the letters. Soon after, I met my pen pal in person for the first time and was gifted a book called *Blue*. We read the book together and to this day I have all our letters and books kept with me. As a young child, I watched my older sister and others present about topics like educational disparities and the language barriers within schools. Little did I know I would grow into investigating similar topics as I grew up. I remember sitting in my first session with CARE, not understanding anything, but soon I understood it as a place to learn, explore, and research in a safe place. It was a space where everyone was family and every session, we would all have larger conversations that consisted of laughter, grief, and hope. One of the first projects I did with CARE was the "Physical Conditions of School." I remember falling in love with research through interviewing my teachers about stories I would have never heard otherwise. It was this project that I shared in one of my first conferences and had the opportunity to publicly speak. I was never into talking in front of big crowds, yet being able to show what I have found and propose solutions was absolutely a joy. I then went on to talk about critical race theory and race and racism in classrooms, and I was even more invested than before. Our team had created pamphlets to hand out to real teachers in their classrooms which made me ecstatic that teachers actually wanted to hear what we had to say and make change.

The meaning of Community-Based Research is all about CARE to me. We took the districts' broken promises to our parents and used our youth voices not only to uplift our parents' voices but to uplift all the voices in the community who were struggling with the same issue. It made me realize the importance of my voice and how important it was for me to stand up since we have power. CARE's lasting words that I always will remember in the deep of my heart is that "Home travels with you. It's never just one place." I realize this because as people continue to grow and move, everyone in the CARE community still stays together like one big family, a family that keeps growing.

Through CARE I was able to explore my interests in filmmaking, grow my writing skills through creative writing, and understand the true meaning of family watching everyone helping one another grow in all ways possible. It is a community that always makes me feel that anything I have accomplished is validated and every growth I've made is valuable. CARE has really shaped me into who I am today because I have applied my learning to my school with public speaking and research and made me fall in love with working with communities around Philadelphia, in addition to motivating me to create such a beautiful space for others.

– Jasmine Lie, youth researcher

Community-based research has meant working to ensure that all members involved in a project are learning from one another and growing beside each other. It is a way in which university researchers collaborate with community researchers, maximizing the knowledge gained from both groups.

Throughout my lovely time with the CARE initiative, I've had the ability to work on various inquiries that have expanded the ways in which I go about asking questions, evaluating situations, and taking action. Some of these projects include my introductory inquiry on how we as a community can work together to stop xenophobia and create safer spaces for one another.

In terms of how the CARE initiative has supported me where I am today, I have to start with how the grandiose amount of support they provided me when I was applying to universities to further my education, from actually assisting me by reading my college application essays, to providing me the emotional support that was needed seeing that I didn't have any family to assist me with the process. I think that the CARE initiative has given me a real opportunity to shape myself into more of a leader. Having the opportunity to be a research fellow involved in the planning and execution of our meetings was a magnificent experience! When it comes to my community as well as the extracurricular activities I am involved in (political organizing, clubs, etc.), I believe that because of the CARE Initiative, I have a more open-minded and community-centered mindset.

A lot of the impact of CARE I feel is not as quantifiable but is just as important. For example, a lot of people who have been a part of the group have gone on to engage in research and advocacy. The group that has really helped me come out of my shell, which is especially important as I go into governmental advocacy and poverty alleviation work.

– Zion Sykes, youth researcher

In schools and society we talk a lot about research that is done in the community. But I'm also thinking about how I can help research be led by my community, and how to make it accessible to my community. And use it as a tool for change, to actually create change and action.

– Olivia Vazquez Ponce, community leader, activist, and Philadelphia teacher

Esta es la oportunidad que tenemos. A pesar de que tenemos distintas lenguas, distintas culturas, nuestras preocupaciones al final del día siguen siendo las mismas. Entonces estamos unidos con las mismas inquietudes y estamos dispuestos a trabajar en un mismo camino todos. A pesar de que todos estamos entre comillas en diferentes lugares, llegamos a un camino donde nos unimos todos por un mismo trabajo, con un mismo sentir. Como minorías no me gustaría sentirnos excluidos, ya que la educación de nuestros hijos es de suma importancia y el idioma no debe ser una barrera para que nos incluyan.

[This is the opportunity we have. Even though we have different languages, different cultures, our preoccupations at the end of the day remain the same. So we are united with the same concerns and we are willing to work on the same path, all of us, even though we may be in "different" places, we reach a path where we all join together for the same work, with the same sentiment. As minorities I would not like for us feel excluded in schools, since the education of our children is of upmost importance and language should not be a barrier for us to be included.]

– Olivia Ponce, community leader, activist, and mother of two

Index

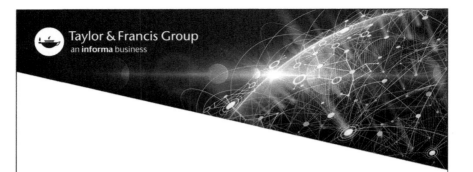